A *Lion* and a *Lamb*

ISBN 978-1-932898-73-6
e. 3

Published by:
Spring Creek Book Company
P.O. Box 1013
Rexburg, Idaho 83440

www.springcreekbooks.com

Cover design © Spring Creek Book Company

All photographs on the cover and in the interior are used courtesy of the Palmyra Bean Packer Collection, except where otherwise noted.

Printed in the United States of America
10 9 8 7 6 5 4 3 2 1
Printed on acid-free paper

Library of Congress Cataloging-in-Publication Data

Packer, Rand H.
  A lion and a lamb : the true story of a young couple's 24-year mission to return the LDS church to its birthplace / by Rand H. Packer.
    p. cm.
  ISBN 978-1-932898-73-6 (pbk. : alk. paper)
  1. Bean, Willard Washington, 1868-1949. 2. Bean, Rebecca. 3. Mormons--Biography. 4. Mormons--New York (State)--History. 5. Palmyra (N.Y.)--Church history. 6. Church of Jesus Christ of Latter Day Saints--New York (State)--History. 7. Mormon Church--New York (State)--History. 8. Smith, Joseph, 1805-1844--Homes and haunts--New York (State). I. Title.

BX8693.P33 2007
289.3092'2--dc22
[B]
                    2007016412

To my angel mother, Palmyra,
from whose lips I first heard the name Joseph Smith,
and of the appearance of the Father and the Son
in a grove called sacred.

The feature film "The Fighting Preacher"
by director T.C. Christensen is based
on the events described in this book.

ACKNOWLEDGMENTS

I am not the first author to write of Willard and Rebecca Bean, nor shall I be the last. Their contributions to the Church and its progress cannot be measured, and I am deeply indebted to them and the heritage they have left. Both Willard and Rebecca's writings and talks, now part of historical record, have been invaluable in preserving many of the events of Church history that happened in Western New York from 1915-1939. I seek to honor them with this work.

The input of Palmyra Bean Packer, now in her 91st year, has been an inspiration. Almost daily I have visited her personally or talked with her on the phone seeking her recollections and remembrances of her life on the Joseph Smith farm. She, for the moment, is a living testimony of the events written in this book.

I extend appreciation to my son, Cameron J. Packer, whose previous interest, research, and scholarly writings have brought accuracy and inspiration to this work.

Dr. Larry C. Porter, one of the finest historians ever, has been my hero over the years and has both directly and indirectly contributed to the writing of this book. Likewise, the staff of Special Collections of the Harold B. Lee Library at Brigham Young University have provided wonderful assistance. Cory Maxwell of Deseret Book Company has also provided initial encouragement and suggestions that have helped make this book a reality.

And this book could not have been written without the kind help and assistance of Bonnie J. Hays, Executive Director of Historic Palmyra. She has generously provided information and visuals that the author was not aware of. She is truly a treasure.

Chad Daybell and his staff at Spring Creek Book Company have been absolutely refreshing and pivotal in bringing this book to daylight. I shall ever be grateful for their expertise and professionalism.

And finally, my beloved wife and sweetheart, Shirlee, whose much-needed encouragement and suggestions made something good much, much better. Now and the future takes on eternal splendor because of her.

INTRODUCTION

Willard and Rebecca Bean

This is a love story. It is true and it really happened. The pictures you will see and the events you will read about are a matter of historical record, most of which take place in the small village of Palmyra, New York. However, this is not your typical love story between a man and a woman, though that is certainly part of it. It reaches far more into the universe than Willard and Rebecca Bean's feelings for each other.

It is true that these two newlyweds had a unique and powerful relationship with each other. It was said of them:

"Those who have never known the deep intimacy, the intense companionship of happy and mutual love, have missed the greatest thing that life has to offer . . . an intimacy that is united by the Holy Spirit of Promise. Those who have never felt this companionship, never can feel the best thing in life. Who gave us this? The Lord Jesus Christ did. This couple had that. They had to have it. They were all alone with their little family there."[1]

Willard and Rebecca's love for each other would give birth to four children within the walls of the Joseph Smith home. It was there that love would abound, strong enough to chase away the tears of adversity that come when nobody likes you.

This is also a love story of a man and a woman who loved someone else even more than they loved each other. They both possessed an unshakable and irrefutable love for the Lord and Savior Jesus Christ. They became acquainted with Him intimately and learn to trust in Him explicitly. They came to know that by loving Him, they in turn ended up loving each other more than they ever could otherwise.

Lastly, this is a love story between two groups of people, those who were members of The Church of Jesus Christ of Latter-day Saints, and those who were not. The forgotten legend of every land is that we all have a Father in Heaven, the great God of the universe, whose children we are. We have forgotten that Heavenly Father loves all of His children, and that we are literally brothers and sisters in a very real sense, regardless of belief or culture.

The life of Willard and Rebecca Bean is a testament to the world that two people in love can make a difference. When love is chosen over hate, then Sunni can sit down with Shiite, black and white are seen as equal, Jew and Moslem embrace, and Christian or Buddhist or Hindu can all say, '*Welcome, we are glad you are here.*'

---

[1] Don B. Colton, *Willard W. Bean Funeral Transcript*, 1949.

PREFACE

Hatred is a powerful darkness. It makes normal people froth at the mouth like hungry wolves, changing their true identities. It separates reason and sanity from the soul and serves as the agent for adoption into the house of the adversary. Hate is the nature, disposition, and personality of the evil one and is capable of turning the softest of men and women into raging beasts with cement hearts.

People of God are no strangers to hatred. Over the centuries hatred has found easy prey amongst good people in every land. They have tasted persecution and martyrdom and have been lured to hate those who hated them first. Hate plus hate equals more hate, which multiplies exponentially into peoples, nations, and cultures hating each other simply because parents hated before them. This evil cycle continues through millennia unless someone, somewhere, stands courageously and refuses to hate back in return, even at the peril of their lives.

Such courage was the lot and mission of Willard and Rebecca Bean, called by a prophet of God in 1915 to serve a wonderful people who had inherited lies and false ideas about The Church of Jesus Christ of Latter-day Saints. This is their story.

Willard Bean, The Mormon Cyclone, preparing to box.

"I always feel reluctant about relating or writing my own experiences, lest it be interpreted as boastful. And yet on the other hand when others tell my experiences they only get it about half right. But if I accomplished anything worthwhile during my sojourn in New York, it is only another evidence that the Lord can yet use the 'weak and foolish things of the world' to accomplish His purposes, and I pass the credit and praise on to Him whom it belongs.

"I was there not to get rich in this world's goods, but to break down prejudice and make friends for Joseph Smith and the Mormon Church. When attacked I fought back fearlessly and courageously pulling no punches. And then when my opponent, in debate or the squared ring, took the count or acknowledged defeat, I would take him by the hand and make a friend of him. I am one of the common people (the common herd) but am not a stranger to the Bible, and with the Lord's help can defend THE GOSPEL against our maligners."

— Willard Bean

As much as possible, the written dialogue is the exact words spoken by the individual. The rest of the dialogue is created by the author to allow adequate expression and description of the event.

CHAPTER 1

"Hey, hey, you over there by the fence line, what do ya think you're doin'?"

Willard Bean turned toward the hateful voice yelling at him and his wife Rebecca from across the field. Willard watched fearlessly as the man waved a shotgun in the air and ran toward them, sputtering a stream of angry words. Willard instinctively moved between his sweetheart and the approaching man, readying himself for a fight. He held his ground as the angry man stopped short of the horse and buggy where Rebecca had chosen to stand.

"You must be those Mormons that moved into the old Smith place," growled the assailant.

"We are, and we just wanted to climb to the top of the hill, if that's all right?"

"It ain't all right, and there ain't no Mormon gonna set foot on that hill," yelled the man as he brandished his shotgun in Willard's face. "Now why don't ya climb back in that buggy of yours and git outta here before I do some real damage to ya?"

Willard knew his body was no match for buckshot and was content to bide his time until the two of them were more equally matched.[1]

"We'll be on our way, then, but first I would like to thank you for this warm welcome you have given us to your friendly

---
[1] Rebecca Bean, tape recording, Palmyra Bean Packer Collection.

village of Palmyra. We had heard that it would be much worse, but you have given us hope and renewed our faith in humanity. We are Willard and Rebecca Bean, and we are happy to be your new neighbors."

The man stood speechless and puzzled as Willard helped his wife up into the buggy and casually joined her. Willard popped the whip above the horse's head, causing the buggy to lurch forward, putting some distance between the two men. The yelling had stopped.

Willard Bean's horse and buggy at the base of the Hill Cumorah.

"Welcome to Palmyra, dear," Willard said. "Believe it or not, he is one of the more friendly ones. But don't worry, we will yet climb to the top of Cumorah. You'll see."

They smiled at each other as the buggy moved briskly through the March wind toward their home. The Joseph Smith farm was not the most alluring and romantic place for a newlywed couple, but the farm had real meaning to Willard and Rebecca, because their faith took wing from this very spot of ground. It was here that the young Joseph Smith had lived and walked and breathed. To the west a short distance was the small grove of trees where he knelt in prayer and split the heavens after centuries of darkness. Here the great God of Heaven, with His Son, had appeared to Joseph and answered the forever-pounding questions of religion.

The soft and steady sound of the horse's gait made it easy for them to become lost in their thoughts as they rode along together. Willard would never forget that weekend in early February 1915, at the Richfield Stake Conference. The meeting house was filled to overflowing with enthusiastic members hoping to see President Joseph F. Smith, who was presiding at the conference.

As Willard entered, he noticed his bride of a few months sitting in the choir. She had a beautiful and wholesome countenance, a gift to her from her Scandinavian heritage. Her sterling qualities and her domestically inclined ambitions were equaled only by the spiritual wealth she guarded inside. She was heaven-sent, he was sure, to fill the void left by the departure and death of his first wife, who left him with two young children. How blessed he felt to have her. After all, he was forty-six, and she was half his age at twenty-three. Willard continued to gaze upon her in the choir seats as President Smith rose to the pulpit and addressed the congregation.

"Willard Bean, will you please come to the stand?"

Willard was shocked to hear his name and was not sure he had heard correctly, but since all of the eyes in the congregation turned his direction he thought he better do as the prophet had requested. As Willard arrived on the stand, President Smith greeted him with a firm handshake and pulled him close.

"Willard, I've got another mission for you. After this service is over, I'll tell you all about it."[2]

Willard heard very little of what was said during the meeting as his mind danced wildly with the prophet's invitation

---

[2] *Autobiography of Willard Washington Bean*, p. 102.

of another mission call. Following the meeting, he caught a glance from Rebecca and motioned for her to meet him in the side foyer. As she approached he could tell she was nervous and filled with uncertainty.

"Willard, what was that all about when President Smith started the meeting? What did he say to you?"

"He wants to see both of us. He said something about a mission."

"A mission!" whispered Rebecca. "You've already served three missions and we're just barely married!"

"I know, I know. I'm as surprised as you are."

It was not long before President Smith entered the hallway and started toward them. Walking next to him, arm-in-arm, was George Albert Smith of the Quorum of the Twelve.

"Willard, Willard Bean," President Smith said. "It is so nice to see you again. And Sister Bean, I have not as yet had the privilege of meeting you. My, aren't you something. I was so happy to hear of your marriage. Come with me and let's slip into this side room for a few minutes. I have something to say to you both."

President Smith carried on in pleasant and friendly conversation as he became more acquainted with Rebecca. It was her first experience being in such close proximity with a prophet of God, feeling his love and interest in her. She enjoyed listening as her husband and this man of God exchanged laughter and reminiscences of the past.

"I'm sure those were wonderful years living in the Manti Temple and taking care of President Daniel H. Wells. Let's see now, Willard, how many baptisms for the dead did you perform without leaving the font?"

"Over eleven hundred, it was," Willard said with a laugh.[3]

"That has to be a record," President Smith said.

[3] Rebecca P. Bean, Fireside Talk, 1964.

It was as though President Smith had all the time in eternity and there was no hurry about him. Rebecca could have listened forever. Then President Smith's warm and loving eyes suddenly became very serious.

"Willard, I want you to listen carefully to me, please. In 1907, without any fanfare, the Church purchased the Joseph Smith farm in Palmyra, New York. We are just now able to take possession of it. We need someone to live there, take care of the farm, and re-establish the Church in that area. When you stepped through the door today, the impression was so strong it was just like a voice said to me, 'There's your man!'[4] I am extending a call to you and Rebecca to serve as missionaries and caretakers of the Joseph Smith farm."

That moment, face-to-face with a prophet of God, was etched forever in the sinew of their souls. The fact that they were both now riding in a buggy toward the farm after being chased off the Hill Cumorah at gunpoint was proof enough that this was not just a scary dream.

Newlyweds Willard and Rebecca Bean in 1915.

While Willard's mind had been deep in the memories of the past several weeks, Rebecca had other things rolling through her mind and stomach. With a huge sigh and a little bit of courage, she sought to complicate his life a little more.

"Willard, were any of Joseph Smith's family born in the Smith home?"

"I really don't know," Willard answered. "Why?"

---

[4] Rebecca P. Bean, Fireside Talk, 1964.

Rebecca said nothing for a long time before saying, "Oh, I just think it would be fun to know."

"I'll try and find out," Willard said. "I think I have some books at home that can give us the answer."

"Willard, do you know of any good doctors in Palmyra?" Rebecca asked. "I haven't been feeling too well lately. It's like my stomach is at constant war with my head. Nothing tastes good anymore."

"I'm sorry, dear. I didn't know you have felt so poorly. Maybe it's the water, or just the change in location. Sometimes that's happened to me as I have moved around from one place to another. It takes a little time for our bodies to adjust to the change."

"Willard," smiled Rebecca as she shook her head in disbelief, "trust me, this has never happened to you. And I'm not going to get over it for about another six months."

It was Willard's turn to remain silent. It only took a quarter of a mile or so for him to decipher Rebecca's cryptic clues.

"Rebecca!" Willard yelled as he pulled back fiercely on the reins. "Are you . . . are we?"

"We are," Rebecca said happily. "I'm sure of it, sometime in August."

"Yes!" Willard bellowed as he stood in the buggy.

"Willard!" hushed Rebecca as she reached up and pulled him back down. "Someone will hear you."

"Of course they'll hear me. That's the idea."

Willard inched closer to Rebecca as he wrapped the horse reins in his left hand and surrounded her with his right arm.

"Think of it, Rebecca. We've only been here for a few weeks and we're about ready to add to the Mormon population in Western New York without even having a baptism."

"Well, we're not quite ready yet," smiled Rebecca. "At least I'm not."

30. GENERAL VIEW OF THE FARM. ROAD FROM MANCHESTER PALMYRA   JOSEPH SMITH FARM, PALMYRA, N. Y.

Looking north to the Joseph Smith Farm, as it would
appear traveling from the Hill Cumorah.

As Willard tethered the horse and buggy in front of the Smith home, he noticed a ragged-looking message nailed to the front door. Rebecca was too busy shaking and folding the blankets to see Willard run to the front door and quickly crumple the note in his hand and force it into his pocket before returning.

"Let me help you in, dear. Then I'll take care of the rig."

Rebecca enjoyed the extra attention and kindness Willard was showing. He was trying so hard, and it meant a lot to her that he was excited about her new condition. As they got to the front porch, Willard turned and embraced her gently.

"The last month has been a real whirlwind, hasn't it?"

"It truly has," sighed Rebecca. "Who would have ever thought that we would be standing here in each other's arms on the front porch of Joseph Smith's home? I still can't believe we are here."

Rebecca pulled back slightly so she could look into Willard's eyes and softly brought her hand to his face.

"Willard, I feel so inadequate. I have never been on a mission before. I don't even know what to say or what to do."

"You'll be fine," comforted Willard, "just fine."

"Oh, I truly hope so. All I know is the Lord wants us here for some reason and that His prophet has called us to serve. I will give everything I have. Just be patient with me as I learn."

Willard held her close and felt the inner strength of this wonderful woman in his arms. Her words reminded him of her quiet strength and inner peace, and the reason he loved her so much.

"You're wonderful," he whispered in her ear. "I'll be in as soon as I take care of the rig."

As Willard led the horse and buggy to the barn he pulled a crumpled piece of paper from his pocket. Keeping it hidden from Rebecca was merely to protect her. It would have worried her so, and she didn't need that. He stared at the words on the paper.

BEWARE OF THE MORMONS
$5000—OFFERED BY THE
ANTI-MORMON LEAGUE [5]

Darkness was ready to play.

---

[5] *Willard Washington Bean Scrapbook*, BYU Special Collections, microfilm.

CHAPTER 2

Willard rose early the following morning. He planned to spend almost the entire day in the barn repairing the farm equipment the Church had inherited with the purchase of the Joseph Smith farm. Spring planting was just around the corner and there was much to do to get the farm ready to become a self-sustaining enterprise. They knew before they came that the Church would give them very little assistance. By the sweat of their brow they would live and by their own initiative and self-reliance they would exist. They knew that God had called them and that He would help them. But they also knew that God never does that which His children can do for themselves.

The seeds of wheat, beans, oats, and barley were already purchased and stored in huge bags in one corner of the home. Peas, cabbage, and celery would be the first seeds planted, with the others to follow.

Horses, dairy cows, sheep, geese, ducks, and chickens added the smells and sounds of life as it was truly meant to be. Willard loved to fill his lungs with the aroma of agriculture. Seeds and hay, soil and livestock and iron, and a myriad of other smells brought back good memories from Willard's youth. He was comfortable with his lot.

Willard ran his finger along the blade of the plow as he eyed the bright silver edge he had just beveled with his metal file. He winced momentarily as the edge cut slightly into his finger, drawing a trace of blood.

The Bean children feeding chickens on the Smith farm.

"All right, I think you're sharp enough to turn a row or two of any soil in this here state," he said as he dropped the file in his large wooden tool box. Willard often carried on conversations with the tools and equipment as did most farmers. He lifted the newly sharpened plow and placed it below the bridle rack on the wall.

"Of course," Willard said, "you know that the soil around Cumorah here is some of the richest in all the land, having been graced with the blood of two civilizations." Willard believed devoutly that both the Nephite and Jaredite nations had fought great wars on this very soil, and that every square foot was rich in history and substance.

"But you, my fine harrow, will take the plowed soil and break it to pieces and ready it for seed, and the miracle of growth."

He stared at the harrow on the floor of the barn, comprised of a huge rake that was the size of four doors put together, with numerous iron tines thrust downward toward the earth. It was a wonderful invention, yet dangerous to use. Soon he would hitch it to his plow horse and stand upon it as he raked the furrowed rows turned up by his plow. Back and forth he would ride, turning hard and rigid gobs of earth into soft and finite particles ready for seed and something worthwhile. How he wished that people, hard and rigid, could somehow be harrowed and made worthwhile.

"Perhaps that's why I'm here," Willard mused. "Maybe I'm a clod buster."

The sun was just disappearing over the western sky as Willard finished buttoning his shirt and putting on a light coat. A hot bath after a hard day's work was always welcome, and now he would sit in his comfortable, cushioned chair and read the few pieces of mail placed on the table next to where he was sitting.

Rebecca waited for him to get comfortable, and then arose from her chair where she had been knitting comfortably for the past twenty minutes. "Feels like we might have an early spring, if the ground hogs are any indication," she said. "I saw them out warming in the sun today."

"I think we're ready, Sweetheart, as soon as heaven allows. The plows are as sharp as they have ever been."

Rebecca paused behind where Willard was sitting, placed her hands on his shoulders, and began to massage his neck.

"I think I will take you with me all day tomorrow," sighed Willard, "and the next day after that, and the next. That way I could get no work done at all. Then again, maybe I . . ."

Willard was unable to finish speaking as a loud knock sounded on the front door. He arose from his chair and looked at Rebecca. "Are we expecting anyone?"

"Not that I know of," she answered.

"Circle the calendar," he quipped. "Today we have our first visitors."

It was not unusual to have visitors call after sundown, but it was certainly not the norm. Most people in the area were farmers who rose early to jumpstart the day—and went to bed early to jump the jumpstart.

Willard opened the door and saw three men standing there. "Gentleman, welcome. Would you please come in?"

"No, we don't want to come in," the lead visitor said. "We think it best if you came outside. We'll do our talkin' out here."

Willard gave Rebecca a cautious glance to comfort her, then he fearlessly stepped outside. Rebecca watched from behind the screen door and listened.

"Gentleman, my name is Willard Bean and I am happy to make your acquaintance," he said, extending his hand to greet them. Willard's hand caught only air, along with cold, demeaning glares from the visitors.

"We know who you are," growled the self-imposed leader of the group. "We'll say our piece, Mr. Bean, and be gone."

Willard slowly retracted his outstretched hand and waited.

"We've held a meeting this evening of citizens of this community, and it is the unanimous feeling of everyone who lives here that you are to leave Palmyra," the man said. "We drove you out of here years ago and you're not coming back. So you best get on your way."

Willard's eyes were fixed calmly upon the three visitors, then he looked at the ground as he pondered an appropriate response to their command. The venom of their remarks meant nothing to a man who had never been afraid of anybody. He had experienced this kind of hatred many times before and knew whose bidding they were doing. A soft smile came across his face as he looked back up at them and caught their focused glare.

"Now, I am sorry to hear that," Willard said. "We had hoped to come out here and fit in with you people and be an asset to this community. We hold no ill feelings toward you for what your people did to us eighty years ago. It was wrong, and always will be. Now you listen to me. We are here to stay, even if we have to fight our way. I'll take you on one at a time or three at a time. It's up to you!"[1]

Willard stood boldly and awaited their response. There had been no variance in his voice or fear in his countenance. This was not calculated rhetoric or the bluff of a frightened victim. He meant what he had said and was ready to back it up.

Stunned by Willard's reply, the three men looked at each other in disbelief as Willard removed his coat, clenched his fists, and assumed his fighting position. To their credit, the trio wasted no time as they turned and headed quickly north.

Little did they know that Willard was a gifted boxer and had once won the middleweight championship of the United States by defeating Bob Douglas in a bout held in St. Louis, Missouri.[2] There was steel in the fists of Willard Bean. Those who fought him in the ring most often had to be helped or carried from it. He stood only 5'9" tall, but there was not one ounce of misdirected flesh on his body. Every muscle was honed and rippled to produce maximum output. He was an absolute physical specimen and could throw a punch clear into the next county.

Willard watched as the men quickly vanished into the darkness where they were more comfortable, then he picked up his coat and stepped up onto the front porch where Rebecca had been watching.

"Oh, Willard, do you think you might have been too strong with them, too bold perhaps?"

He shook his head. "We must establish our position and they must know we are not afraid. The Lord has not called

[1] Rebecca P. Bean, *An Account of the Palmyra Missionary Experiences of Willard W. Bean and Rebeca P. Bean*, 1964, Palmyra Bean Packer Collection, 2.
[2] David F. Boone, *Palmyra Revisited: The New York Mission of Willard W. Bean*, Regional Studies of LDS Church History, 127.

Willard Bean in 1894.

us here to turn our backsides and run for cover. He has sent us here, and here we will stay. We will not be driven out again."

She knew he was right. She was just not used to this kind of battle. She was so grateful for him, his protective and powerful nature, and his relentless courage and sense of duty. He was all she was not, and she was glad he was at her side.

As the weeks and months of loneliness grew, so did Rebecca's waistline. The summer had been fruitful in the field and the warmth of August made ready for the harvest and also for the birth of their first child.

But among the people of Palmyra, the air was cold. Rebecca sought endlessly for a nurse to stay in the home and to assist in the birth of her child, but the answer was always the same. "Go back to Salt Lake City, where you belong," she was told. "No one around here is going to help you. I wouldn't dare come into your home. Go get Joe Smith's angel to come help you."

Willard was prepared to deliver the baby by himself. He had delivered many calves and horses over the years and felt confident he could do the same with one of his own. But this was Rebecca's first child and she naturally felt and longed for the assurance of motherly experience and skill.

Rebecca felt the sting of prejudice and the helplessness of her condition. She had never imagined that Christians could treat Christians in such a way. Each night she would cry and plead with the Lord that someone would be sent to help her. She knew it was not the people's fault and did not blame them. The father of lies had done his work well and the people were only doing what they thought was right.

But in early August an angel knocked on the door of the Joseph Smith home. A young woman stood on the porch and said, "Mrs. Bean, I understand you have been trying to find a nurse to help you with the delivery of your baby."

"Yes, that is right," Rebecca said. "I have tried for several weeks to find someone, but nobody feels comfortable helping us because of who we are."

"I'm not a trained nurse," the woman said, "but I have attended a lot of situations like this. I would be happy to help. I am also not afraid to come into a Mormon's home. I know you are good people. My brother was curious about the Mormons

*Summer crops in the fields between the Joseph
Smith home and the Sacred Grove.*

and went to Salt Lake City to see for himself. He enjoyed it so much he decided to stay there. He told me all the bad stuff I had heard about the Mormons was all a bunch of lies and not to believe it. So here I am, and I will be happy to help in any way I can."[3]

"Oh, thank you, thank you, thank you," Rebecca said as her eyes began to moisten with tears. "You will never know what this means to me. The baby is due any day now and we have a room upstairs you can stay in. We will provide for all of your needs while you are here."

"I live on a farm further south here on Stafford Road. I will go back home and pack my things and be back this afternoon. Now don't you worry, Mrs. Bean. Everything is going to be just fine."

Rebecca closed the screen door, found the nearest chair and cautiously sat down. This young lady was the first friendly face she had spoken to since she arrived months ago. She permitted her tears to flow more readily now as she contemplated what had just occurred. She smiled as she remembered reading in the Book of Mormon a few days before about the Lamanites eternal hatred toward the Nephites, all because the parents had taught their children to hate.

She opened the book and read again of the great King Zeniff sending spies out among the Lamanites. She read his words in Mosiah 9:1 that "when I saw that which was good among them I was desirous that they should not be destroyed."

Rebecca thought of her own situation. "These are good people we are living with," Rebecca said to herself. "If they will let us live with them a while, they will know that we are good people, too. They might even learn to like us."

True to her word, the young lady returned in the afternoon

---

[3] Rebecca Bean, Fireside Talk, 1964.

and spent the next three weeks assisting in the birth and care of Rebecca and her new baby daughter. The woman, Ethel Hack, left as suddenly as she came when Rebecca was back on her feet again, her saintly service completed. Rebecca would never forget Ethel's courageous kindness. Her assistance had been a direct answer to Rebecca's prayers.

Rebecca and Willard had been so busy bringing life and harvesting the farm that they had scarcely had time to name their daughter.

"Perhaps another Joseph or Hyrum would be fitting," Willard suggested slyly.

"How about an Emma, or Lucy, or Priscilla," Rebecca responded with a laugh.

They finally decided on a name. No one in western New York was quite ready for the name given to the first member of the Mormon Church born there in over eighty years.

Her name would be Palmyra.

CHAPTER 3

When Palmyra Bean was born on August 15, 1915, she joined the two children, Phyllis and Paul, from Willard's previous marriage, in bringing a little more noise to the farm. In the short time the Beans had been there, they had come to love the place and also the people, even though they felt no reciprocation from the community.

Some of the people joked about the baby's name, but many were touched that a Mormon couple would name a child after their fair city, and found themselves wondering why they had not thought to do the same themselves. But years of hatred did not vanish simply because of a little girl's name. The ongoing darkness continued to conspire against them.

One day, Willard told Rebecca, "I must go to town for supplies and think it will take the better part of the day and into the night before I can get home. I'll probably have to go to Macedon, since they are not willing to sell us

Willard, Rebecca, and Palmyra, 1916

much here yet. It's best you not wait up for me, dear."

Rebecca tried to appear undaunted by her husband's words, but Willard sensed her anxiety about being alone. "Sweetheart, you need not worry so," he said. "All will be well with us. I know it will."

He bent down as he folded his supply list into his shirt pocket and kissed his wife and his precious little Palmyra. Willard didn't like leaving his family alone, but they were not yet ready to make the all-day journey with him. He had learned over the years to trust in the protective hands of God when on His errand and owed his very existence to that principle.

Rebecca watched from the doorway as Willard popped the whip over the head of Old Brownie. The buggy lurched forward and then gradually disappeared up Stafford Road toward Palmyra. It was the middle of October and the bright leaves of fall still clung to the tree branches. Rebecca felt a chill in the air as she began her domestic chores that never seemed to end.

Upon arriving in town, Willard headed directly for the harness shop in search of some parts for the damaged singletree he had wired together on his buckboard. He knew it would be a challenging experience, but he felt up to it. He opened the door briskly and marched directly to the counter where several men had gathered for their morning coffee and social hour. Silence reigned as everyone stopped talking and stared at their city's most-disliked resident. Willard decided to enjoy the attention and make the best of it.

"Good day, gentlemen," he said. "I am in need of some parts for a singletree and I am wondering if you might have some available?"

A large man stepped forward who appeared to be the store owner. He told Willard, "We do have those parts, but they're not for sale at this particular time."

"I see," Willard said. "Can you give me some idea as to the particular time they might be available?"

"Well, I can't really say," the store owner said. "I suspect it all hinges on who's wantin' to buy it."

"Well, as I mentioned, I'm the one that's needing it, so I reckon that I'll be the one buying it."

"Well then," the man said, "it's not for sale. We're pretty particular here."

"That's fine," Willard answered. "I'll just pick one up in Macedon this afternoon. They're not quite as particular over there. Thanks anyway."

Willard walked out of the store into the sunlight and smiled as he headed to the blacksmith to see if his luck would change. He enjoyed walking down the streets of civilization, noticing the shops and the latest contributions to society spawned from the avenues of New York City. But his walks always came with a price. Whenever he was in town he became a public spectacle. The constant looks, stares, and taunting comments had become customary and they bothered him very little. He had faced them all of his life.

The October sun had chased away any thought of winter as Willard strolled along in front of the well-kept homes on Main Street. Suddenly, without warning, Willard found himself the target of a deluge of water, compliments of a local home-owner who had turned his watering hose in Willard's direction.

"I understand you Mormons believe in baptism by immersion," hollered the belligerent man, not understanding the nature of the fighter he was about to engage. In an instant, Willard had acrobatically leapt over the picket fence that separated them and grabbed the man by the shirt collar with both hands.

"Yes," Willard said with a smile, "and we also believe in the laying on of hands."[1] The man wondered if he would ever water his yard again as he found himself cowering beneath this fighting Mormon machine. Although Willard was not given to violence or using his God-given talents for anything except the furtherance of God's work, it was his nature to defend himself and the Church with his brawn and knuckle power.

In contrast, Rebecca relied on other forms of help for protection and for moving the work of the Lord along. That evening, an obnoxious knock sounded at the door. It increased in intensity, even after Rebecca had already opened the door. She noticed the porch was completely filled with men, accompanied by five women.

"We are ministers," they curtly proclaimed, "and these ladies are school teachers. We've been over to Clifton Springs to attend a ministerial convention. We passed Mormon Hill and thought we would come over here and see this place and hear a little about Ole Joe Smith."

Rebecca wondered why people so often referred to the Prophet Joseph as Ole Joe Smith when he was only in his teens and early twenties when he had lived there.

"Please come in," Rebecca said. "My husband is in town, but I would be happy to share with you the story of the Prophet Joseph Smith."

As they entered the front room, Rebecca began to tell the story of the gold plates and the ancient record from Cumorah that was given to him by an angel named Moroni.

"This is the room where the prophet brought the plates and hid them under the hearthstone."

Rebecca pointed to where the fireplace had been and where the hearthstone would have been, but that was all she was able to finish. As though it had been orchestrated from the unseen world, the crowd unleashed their insulting barrage of questions

---

[1] Rebecca P. Bean Talk, Salt Lake City, Utah, February 5, 1966.

for which they sought no answer. Noise and accusations filled the room. They had come only to taunt, to injure, and to hurt.

"How old was this Joe Smith, anyway? Wasn't he a money-digger, a treasure hunter? Where are these gold plates now? Bring them to us so we can see them," they sneered. "Why did Old Joe rob the cradle and kidnap his wife? How many wives did he have, anyway? How many wives does your old man have? Seen any low-flying angels lately?"

Without ceasing the questions roared forth as though a company of cannons had been unleashed. Rebecca felt the darkness invade her home, and her little baby began to cry as the yelling increased and chaos intensified. Fearing for the life of her child and having nowhere to turn but heaven, Rebecca prayed fervently within herself as the visitors gnashed at her from every direction.

Deep down inside she prayed, all by herself, without uttering a word, pleading for help and protection for herself and her little daughter. It took but a moment for heaven to hear, and then quietly, yet powerfully, like the rays of the morning sun, a gentle haze of light pushed its way into the defiant room.

Though she could see no one, Rebecca felt the presence of someone standing beside her. At that moment, everyone in the room went silent, and it was peaceful and calm, much like it was on a sacred morning in the spring of 1820.

Rebecca would later say, "I bear humble testimony that after that I knew the Prophet Joseph Smith. I was able to go on and tell Joseph's story and defend him and tell about his receiving the plates, and they listened. They didn't say anything, anymore. . . . I asked them if they would like to register in the book where we had our visitors write their names, and they did. One or two of them apologized for their behavior and thanked me for what I had told them. Then they went outside.

"I sat down in my rocker. My little baby had dropped off to

sleep and I sat down and meditated over what had happened—
this wonderful feeling that had come into the room and the
knowledge and feeling that someone stood beside me to help
me. And again I say, after that I knew the Prophet Joseph
Smith, and I felt his love and his influence all the years we lived
there."[2]

It was not uncommon during the first few years on the
Smith farm to have passers-by yell from their buggies their
displeasure at having the Beans as their neighbors. Days and
weeks hurried into months and years as Willard's *We're here to
stay*" attitude became a reality.

As the children grew and attended school they assumed the
special chair bolted to the floor in the corner for the Mormon
children, away from the other students. Both Palmyra and her
younger brother, Pliny, were often the brunt of ridicule, stolen
lunches and pernicious pranks. Seldom would they go out in
the schoolyard for recess, for when they did they were always
shunned, and at other times threatened.

During the colder months Willard would often pick the
children up from school in the buggy or sleigh. During the
warmer months, the children would often walk the two miles
home. At times Rebecca would ride with Willard, pick the
children up, and do their weekly shopping while in town. Six
years had made a difference as the merchants recognized that
the money a Mormon spent had just as much value as anyone
else's.

"I'll meet you back here at the buggy in an hour," Willard said
one day as he hoisted three-year-old Pliny upon his shoulders.

"See you in an hour, then," Rebecca responded. "Come,
Palmyra. Let's go buy some girl things."

They passed the four churches heading east on Main

---

[2] Bean, Fireside Talk, 1964.

Street and then waited on the corner of Williams street with some other shoppers as several buggies made their way into the intersection. A small, curly haired little puppy was leashed tightly to its owner as they waited.

"Oh Mamma, look at that cute little puppy," Palmyra said as she knelt down on one knee to engage the playful pup.

"Don't you dare touch that dog, little girl," yelled the lady on the other end of the leash. Snatching the puppy away, she demanded, "Don't you ever touch my dog again!"

The lady added, "I advise you keep better control of your children, woman. No Mormons are allowed to touch any dogs here in Palmyra."

Palmyra stood frozen, clinging to her mother's arm as the lady's rebuke continued. "If I see it happen again, I'll have you reported to the authorities."

Palmyra started to cry as Rebecca gathered her up and carried her across Williams Street to Exchange Row.

"Now don't you cry, my little sweetheart," Rebecca said. "She's not a very happy person, is she? And besides, we have a lot more animals to pet than she does. We'll let her pet our animals if she ever comes to our place and maybe that will make her happy."[3]

A few weeks later, Rebecca heard the front door open and close as little Palmyra entered quietly and ran upstairs to her room. It was quite unlike her usual after-school entrance into the house, so Rebecca walked over to the stairs and peered up the banister. She heard her daughter's muffled sobs. Rebecca quickly climbed the stairs and found a soft place on the side of her daughter's bed.

"Will anyone ever like me, Mamma?" Palmyra asked. "Will I ever have any friends?"

---

[3] Palmyra Bean Packer Interview, August 20, 2006.

With tears streaming down her cheeks she pleaded, "Why can't someone just be nice to me?"

Rebecca, mixing her tears with her little daughter's already moist face, gathered her up in her arms.

"My sweet Palmyra, this is quite a pickle we have put you in, isn't it? I am so sorry we have done this to you and that it is so hard. It is hard for me, too. I don't have any friends either, not one. I just have you, and our little family, and the missionaries and the Church leaders, when they come. That's all we have right now."

Rebecca could feel the silent sobs and warm tears on her neck as she rocked back and forth with her precious little six-year old.

"It will take time, my little one," she continued. "These are really good people and we must give them time to know that we, too, are good people. It will happen, but it will take some time, maybe a long time, but it will happen. God will help us, and if we will try real hard, He will make it happen. I promise you He will."

Rebecca and Palmyra held each other in their arms for a long time and then, without any planning or ceremony, found themselves kneeling at the side of a little bed in the upper room of a home where a young prophet had once knelt when he, too, had no friends.

CHAPTER 4

Little by little the temperature of western New York began to rise a degree or two. The residents of Palmyra began to resign themselves to the fact this little family from Utah had glue in their boots, and that they were stuck with them no matter what. Seldom were the Beans able to talk about the Church to their neighbors, and when they tried they were quickly rebuffed. Instead, street meetings became the way for them to declare the restoration message.

Willard loved to sing, but a bull-moose voice singing the hymns of Israel often sent people scurrying in the opposite direction. He needed sweet music to attract bystanders and soon Rebecca's high soprano tones could be heard at the main intersection in Palmyra. Traffic jams ensued at the intersection and complaints were registered.

This opposition caused Willard to visit with Pliny T. Sexton, a local banker and part-owner of the Hill Cumorah. Willard was forced into remembering the counsel given him by President Smith before they departed on their mission. He was told to make friends, be patient with the people, and to be in no hurry to begin missionary work due to the great prejudice that was still there.

Willard had made friends with Mr. Sexton soon after their arrival, and he would later name his second child, Pliny, in honor of their friendship. Willard asked Mr. Sexton if he might use the park adjacent to his bank to preach. He not only agreed, but offered his own bandstand to use as a pulpit, replacing the apple crate Willard had been using to rest his scriptures on.

Making friends and holding street meetings helped establish the Beans as part of the community, but sharing the gospel moved ahead at a snail's pace. However, Hathaway Brook, used in the early days of the Church for baptisms, would soon again be used for that sacred ordinance.

Early missionaries standing by Hathaway Brook on the Smith Farm.

In 1921, Charles Collins and his wife were baptized, and by August 1923, another young lady was preparing herself for baptism.

Palmyra had just turned eight years old, and plans were made for her baptism to coincide with the upcoming visit of President Heber J. Grant. The prophet would be joined by apostles James E. Talmage, Rudger Clawson, Joseph Fielding Smith, and B.H. Roberts to celebrate the 100th anniversary of Moroni appearing to Joseph Smith.

Rebecca was very pleased that Dr. Talmage would arrive at the Smith Farm in time for Palmyra's baptism. Both she and Willard had enjoyed a close friendship with this vibrant apostle since coming to New York, and when he arrived, Rebecca made a special request. She said, "Dr. Talmage, I would like my little daughter to be confirmed by you. I think that would be something lovely for her to remember, and I would be so pleased with it."

Dr. Talmage peered over his glasses, smiled gently, and said, "President Grant is in charge of the meeting. I hate to make any suggestions, but let's you and I pray about it."[1]

Nothing else was said, and though Rebecca had been praying about it already, she was happy to leave it in the Lord's hands.

The fruits of friendship continued to reap great rewards. The farm of James Inglis bordered the Hill Cumorah and went halfway up the west side. One evening, while Willard was sitting with Mr. Inglis on his front porch looking toward the hill, both men felt the inspiration of the Lord.

"Willard, let me sell you my farm," Mr. Inglis said. "You will then be able to say you own part of the hill at least."

The price seemed reasonable and Willard quickly obtained permission from Church authorities to proceed. However, when the news of the possible sale became public, it was rumored that the wife of Mr. Inglis had persuaded him not to sell to the Church.

Willard soon sat on his friend's front porch again. "Jim, I understand there is some hesitancy in selling us your farm," he said.

"Maybe some are hesitant, but not me," Mr. Inglis said. "I want you to know that I am still master of my own house, and I will still sell you the farm if you will agree to buy all the equipment, horses, cows, and machinery with it."

Following some brief negotiations the deal was finalized and

---

[1] Rebecca Bean, Fireside Talk, 1964.

the Church obtained its first partial possession of the sacred hill. And because of Willard's friendship with banker Pliney T. Sexton, who owned the rest of the Hill Cumorah, members of the Church could once again walk up the sacred slopes where the Prophet Joseph had obtained the gold plates.

The purchase was completed on September 17, 1923, six days before the baptism of little Palmyra. Soon the leaders of the Church would arrive and a memorable missionary conference would be held with meetings both on the Hill Cumorah and in the Sacred Grove.

The missionaries came by foot and train, all 240 of them, tracting on their way, declaring the restored gospel to anyone who would listen. On Saturday, September 22, the day began with a flag-raising ceremony on the north end of the Hill Cumorah. A flagpole held the blue and white Cumorah/Ramah colors in memory of the ancient civilizations once associated with the hill. The colors of the majestic Old Glory also waved in the wind atop the flagpole.

The flag-raising ceremony atop Hill Cumorah on September 22, 1923.

Later in the day the missionaries sat upon the hill's western slope, receiving instruction from their mission president, B.H. Roberts, and others.

President B.H. Roberts preaching on the western slope of the Hill Cumorah.

President Grant and B.H. Roberts leading the march to the Sacred Grove on Sunday morning, September 23, 1923.

It was a glorious day, followed by another glorious day on Sunday wherein they marched to the Sacred Grove under the colors of the United States and held a sacrament meeting.

Later in the day they returned to the Hill Cumorah where President Grant gave a stirring testimony of the Restoration and the Prophet Joseph Smith. Upon the conclusion of President Grant's talk, B.H. Roberts arose and said, "Elders and Sisters, you have heard one of the great testimonies ever born of the Prophet Joseph Smith. And now I ask you if you believe this testimony and if President Grant's testimony is your testimony?"

A mighty and thunderous "yes" rang out in unison from the slopes of Cumorah. Following this affirmation of his testimony President Grant led those present in the sacred "Hosanna Shout" as they worshipped together on a mountain of the Lord. [2]

It was late afternoon when the conference visitors returned to the Smith home. All of the meetings had ended, except one. Palmyra was dressed in white, and waiting.

In recent weeks, Palmyra's prayers for a friend had been answered. Genevieve Morgan and Palmyra had become close friends since her family had come to live in the tenant house on the Smith farm. Willard had found it difficult to care for the farm completely and attend to his other duties and continual missionary conferences being held in the Sacred Grove.

The Morgans were a great help in running the farm and the Beans also found a listening ear to the gospel message. As is always the case, the spirit of truth rings louder than the spirit of antagonism. Three of the Morgan children were ready to be baptized and join Palmyra in becoming members of the Church on her special day.

Willard rose early on the morning of September 23, 1923 and set about the task of preparing the baptismal font. With a shovel in hand and a few logs and large rocks, Willard made his way along the edge of Hathaway Brook meandering silently through the property just west of the Smith home. Quickly a dam was prepared to back the water up sufficiently to produce a small pond deep enough to baptize in, just as it was done for many of the early baptisms in the Church.

When the time came, Palmyra entered the pond with her father and they made their way to the deepest part. Willard

---

[2] *James E. Talmage Journal*, September 23, 1923, BYU Collections.

Palmyra being baptized by her father, Willard Bean. Geneveive
Morgan is standing at the edge of the pond.

raised his right hand, offered the baptismal prayer, and immersed her in the water. When Palmyra came up out of the water and wiped her eyes, little Genevieve was nowhere to be found. As soon as she saw Palmyra immersed, her fear of water overcame her and off she went running. She was not about to go under the water and was found hiding amongst the cars in the field two hours later.

It was nearly two more years before she found the courage to be baptized, and for the next eighty years she and Palmyra continued their friendship through letters and telephone conversations until Genevieve's death in the year 2005.[3]

Following the baptisms, President Grant confirmed young William Morgan, Elder Clawson confirmed his younger sister,

[3] Palmyra Bean Packer Interview, 12 October 2006.

Hazel, and then President Grant said, "I think we will have Dr. Talmage confirm little Palmyra Bean."

Rebecca smiled as Dr. Talmage arose and came forth to do the confirmation. As he passed Rebecca, he smiled back at her in return. She knew that he had prayed about it, and Dr. Talmage knew that she had prayed about it also. Heavenly Father had heard both of their prayers, and they were answered.[4]

But as the Beans began to see and enjoy some of the fruits of their labors, there were other forces at work to discredit, refute, and injure the message and mission of the Church. With the commemorative services at Cumorah being a major focus of the news in western New York and with much positive press, it would only be normal for opposing forces to emerge. Though some ministers were accepting and even friendly to the Beans, others were not and sought to discredit the foundations of Mormonism.

Two ministers and a song leader purported to have uncovered two bronze plates on the slopes of Cumorah, which they claimed were part of the gold plates Joseph Smith had received from Angel Moroni. To them it proved the Church a hoax as they tried to create a negative stir in the community against Willard and the events on Cumorah.

Fortunately, no one seemed to take much notice, and even less noticed when the bronze plates proved to be of recent origin and obviously a poor attempt by someone to discredit the Church.

Willard had experienced this kind of antagonism before, and he rather relished the opportunity to enter the ring in defense of the Church. It was time to lace up his gloves.

---

[4] *James E. Talmage Journal*, September 23, 1923, BYU Collections.

Rochester American Apr. 6, 1930

They Found Mormon Plates

REV. FAY C. MARTIN   REV. CHARLES E.   MELVIN LAWTON
                              DRIVER

DISPUTED—Rev. Mr. Driver, a Methodist evangelist, created something of a stir in 1923 when he unearthed two bronze plates on Cumorah Hill at Palmyra, where the original golden plates bearing the Book of Mormon were found a century ago by Joseph Smith. The Rev. Mr. Martin, pastor of the Church of God, and Melvin Lawton, the evangelist's song leader were with him at the time. Mormons merely scoffed at the find.

*A newspaper article showing the bronze plates reported
to have been discovered on the Hill Cumorah.*

CHAPTER 5

As the years rolled precipitously along, Willard's unrelenting and unyielding defense of the Church became acceptable to the community. He was not afraid to bring his fighting spirit into play and even into a fight, if necessary. The residents began to respect this man of principle who would not back down, and just as a fighter in the ring gains respect for his opponent as the rounds tick by, so it was with the Beans and everyone else. Some of the hatred had finally been replaced with respect.

The local newspapers jumped on the bandwagon and found excellent reading fodder for their subscribers. Names such as *The Fighting Parson, Kid Bean,* and *The Mormon Cyclone* were front-page news in a small community, and Willard maneuvered to take advantage of the newly found press coverage.

Willard loved to compete and to use his God-given talents and gifts to further the work of the kingdom. Always the perfect specimen of physical fitness, he was often asked his secret and motivation to maintaining his physique and agility.

He took great delight in sharing his talents and skills with others and at no charge would tutor private pupils in the art of boxing, juggling, and gymnastics. Weekly classes were held in Palmyra for youth or adults who might be interested in improving their bodies.

"This is my creed," Willard would say. "When the body was entrusted to my care it was perfectly organized. I am supposed to keep it free from all contamination; to keep it pure and

undefiled; to uniformly develop all my faculties and all parts of
my body to their highest capacity, that I may eventually bring
my entire body to a symmetrical shape and the highest stage
of development, approaching as nearly as possible that which
God designed it, a perfect specimen of manhood in the image
of my Maker, filling nature's measurements."[1]

"There is rightly a law," Willard would also say, "against
carrying pistols and other deadly weapons, but there is no
law against carrying science with nature's weapons to defend
yourself against insolent aggression." [2]

He had great confidence in his skills to defend himself
physically, and since most of the male population had dreamed
of legally laying into him with their fists, he sought to oblige
them. He challenged one and all to enter the ring and match
their fighting skills with his. On one occasion challengers filled
the first three rows of the hall, anxious to deck this Mormon
once and for all. One by one they would leave the ring, either
with assistance or unconscious, with very few ever landing a
punch. He did not fear what man could do and he was capable
of punishing anyone who would take him on, regardless of
size.

One day while Willard and his young son Pliny were
stringing fence line around a pasture near the Hill Cumorah,
one of the local farm hands was foolish enough to challenge
the Mormon Elder again. All the filth that one man could say
landed directly in Willard's face. The man, large in stature,
felt safe from any physical attack of the 5' 9" Mormon. As the
filth and accusations increased in intensity, Willard's patience
came to an end. He put down his hammer and approached the
heckler.

[1] *Willard Bean, Scrapbook.*
[2] *Palmyra Courier-Journal, 1929; Willard Bean Scrapbook*

"I've heard just about enough," Willard told the man. "Do you want to leave now, while you are still able, or do you want to spend the rest of the day on your back?"

"I don't see anyone around that can do that," countered the heckler as he stepped toward Willard.

Willard took a step forward and landed his fist squarely on the jaw of the intruder and with one punch laid him out flat on his back, and then returned to continue working on the fence line with his son.[3]

Maybe Willard's personality was exactly what the Lord needed in these very unique and difficult circumstances. Perhaps it was a carry-over from his early missionary days in the Southern States when President J. Golden Kimball cautioned him, "Elder Bean, you've been a fighter all of your life. Things are different now. You must turn the other cheek."

"I'll be happy to turn the other cheek," Willard said, "if they can hit the first one."[4]

It just was not in his nature to back down. Shortly after this counsel from his mission president, while passing out tracts and preaching in the town square, he was confronted by a town bully and leader of the anti-Mormon mob.

"Men, if we strap these preachers across a log and whip them with hickory sticks, they'll remember us a long time."

The crowd, like a pack of hungry wolves ready for the kill, jeered and taunted the missionaries, feeling brave because of their numbers. Willard was born for moments like this. A wry little smile forced its way onto his face.

"Tell you what. Why don't we make this a sporting event," Willard replied. "Just you and me. If I lick you, we preach. If you lick me, you get to whip us."

---

[3] Vicki Bean Topliff, *The Fighting Parson*, 61.
[4] Topliff, *The Fighting Parson*, 12.

The crowd continued to gather as the small Elder Bean prepared to battle the large Goliath of the mob. He found a resting place for his Bible and Book of Mormon on a nearby tree stump.

"Lay there, religion," Willard said, "while I prepare this man for Mormonism."

Willard's boxing savvy made quick and easy work of the large and boisterous leader, who soon found himself not only eating dirt, but the words he had spoken a few moments before. He quickly gained respect for this different kind of man of the cloth and even became an ally to the missionaries.

"Why don't you boys use the local schoolhouse to preach in," came the bully's suggestion, "and me and my boys will see that it is packed every night."[5]

Willard just had a way about him that seemed to turn enemies of the Church into friends. They just couldn't help liking him. His fearless demeanor seemed to rub off on them and they wished they had what he had.

In another instance, while in the home of a non-Mormon on his mission to the Southern States, the owner of the home suddenly took offense at something that was taught.

"I am ordering you off of my land," yelled the angry man, "and all I want to see is your tracks and your heels toward the door."

"That's fine then, sir. I'll be on my way."

Willard turned slightly toward the door and very slowly meandered his way, never quite getting to the other side of the room.

"You have one second to be out of here," shouted the man, "or I'll give you a beating you'll never forget!"

---

[5] Topliff, *The Fighting Parson*, 14.

"All right, if you feel that way about it," Willard said. "You have hatred in your heart, and won't feel good about it until you get rid of it."

Willard never made it to the door. The man lunged at him as Willard maneuvered himself to the side. The man lunged again, but only found air. Willard immediately had him defenseless on the floor and gave him a good spanking. Willard slowly released him and let the man go free. Willard was ready for whatever would come next.

"Ain't nobody ever done that to me before," growled the assailant.

"I just did it!" Willard said. "I mean no harm, but there's no reason to be hateful."

The man stared at Willard for several seconds, pondering his momentary defeat and his next plan of attack. "Have you had supper?" the man asked gruffly.

"No, I haven't, not yet."

"Why don't you stay and have some, then?"

"My companion is out on the highway," Willard said. "Can I bring him?"

"Bring him in, and we'll eat together."

That man joined the Church because he'd never met a man in all his life like Willard Bean.[6]

On another occasion Willard and his companion were accosted by a mob, the leader of which demanded a sign.

"Show us a sign, you Mormon boys. We want to see a sign right now."

"I'll be happy to oblige you with a sign," teased Willard, "but my companion hasn't been out very long and he's not used to such things. Would it be all right if we sent him down the road a piece and then I would be happy to give you a sign."

<hr>

[6] LeGrand Richards, *Funeral Service Transcript of Willard W. Bean*, in possession of the author.

A First-Class Example of Muscular Christianity

WILLARD W. BEAN

Mr. Bean is 60 years young. He still retains much of the vigor of youth. He attributes his present health to consistant living and physical culture. He was an athlete from his early youth and has taught practically all branches of athletics and gymnasium work.

Mr. Bean still keeps an abbreviated apparatus for physical development at his home on the farm, such as boxing gloves, wall exercises, punching bag, Indian clubs, dumb bells, etc. He has discontinued his classes in physical culture in the Grange Hall for the winter, but will resume this work early in the spring. He will continue with his private pupils in boxing and other individual work. Mr. Bean is an example and advocate of muscular Christianity. He says there is rightly a law against carrying pistols and other deadly weapons, but there is no law against carrying science with nature's weapons to defend yourself against insolent aggression.

Newspaper article, probably from the Palmyra Courier-Journal, on Willard's athletic skills.

The leader of the mob accepted his proposition with the nod of his head, and Willard motioned to his companion to start down the road. Willard watched until his companion had about a quarter-mile headstart and then turned to the leader of the mob.

"Here is the sign that I am going to give you," Willard said. "I will strike you blind."

Willard immediately sent a lightning left jab to the bully's eye, followed with a crushing right cross to his other eye. As the ruffian reeled backward, landing hard on the ground, Willard took off running for all he was worth. As he approached his companion, he began to holler, "Run, Elder, run! Run for your life!" And they did.[7]

It did not matter to Willard whether he was living in Tennessee, California or New York. If the gospel needed to be defended, he would gladly do it. However, he was not just a good athlete with muscles and a competitive edge. He could fight with the scriptures as well as any of the trained ministers of his day.

Throughout their stay in western New York, Willard and his family were periodically welcome guests at the various religious denominations throughout the area. His vast knowledge of the scriptures augmented by the restored truths of the gospel gave him more firepower for doctrinal interpretation than anyone else. Often in their Sunday School classes the ministers would ask Willard to expound on different verses.

Jealousy soon prevailed and he was asked by members of the Baptist congregation not to attend their meetings anymore. But the minister insisted that he keep coming.

The minister said, "I have been making inquiries and have come to the conclusion that Mr. Bean is not a polygamist, that

[7] Arien S. Bean, *Story of Willard Washington Bean*, July 20, 2004.

he occasionally comes to our services, and I wish he would come more often."[8]

Two wealthy heiresses then threatened to withdraw their financial support if "that Mormon Polygamist" continued to come, so the Beans graciously removed themselves from the congregation. Within a few days Willard received a phone call from the Presbyterian minister with the invitation to attend their church. He was happy to oblige.

As the light of truth continued to chase away the darkness of intolerance, the adversary stepped up the opposition by bringing in some "paid hirelings" as Willard called them, to spread lies and defamation against the Church. Lulu Loveland Shepherd was sent in by the Christian Reform Association, followed by a Dr. Dodge, Attorney Alexander, and a Mrs. Walker, all with the intent to destroy the Beans and the Church.

Again, Willard's fighting spirit rose to the occasion. He often said, "I did not come to Palmyra to fight other churches, or any man because of his religion or lack of religion. I am naturally a tolerant and peaceable man and hoped to fit in with the better element and work for the moral uplift and betterment of the community. But I have a little fighting blood in my veins and when I or my people are maliciously attacked by character assassins, I feel it not only my privilege, but my duty, to fight back in self-defense."[9]

A local minister, Reverend Martin, challenged some of Willard's beliefs by printing an article in the local newspaper. Willard counter-punched with a newspaper article of his own offering to answer Reverend Martin's questions by using the Reverend's own pulpit. Willard's invitation was rejected as more articles and counter-articles continued to find print in the local newspaper.

[8] Willard Washington Bean Autobiography, 25.
[9] Willard Washington Bean Autobiography, 29.

This ongoing debate excited the community and finally Willard wrote, "Reverend Martin, for some reason, continues to ignore my propositions. I shall try one more. I will rent the Odd Fellows Hall next Sunday afternoon when I shall endeavor to answer his questions. I shall personally bear all the expenses and give Reverend Martin the privilege of replying after I get through. Accordingly, I cordially invite Reverend Martin and his congregation, and others who may be interested, to be present. I shall take up no collection."

Willard spoke to a large audience that evening, but Reverend Martin could not be found. In the following days Reverend Martin presented another article for publication, to which the manager of the newspaper responded, "Mr. Bean has made you every proposition a reasonable man could ask for. You started this controversy with Mr. Bean, but you haven't got the guts to back up your accusations. Better take your article home. If you leave it here, I shall consign it to the waste basket."[10]

Reverend Martin was soon released from his ministerial position, as were others who sought to tangle with this two-fisted, tongue-twisting farmer from Utah.

---

[10] Vicki Bean Topliff, *The Fighting Parson*, 68.

CHAPTER 6

Willard's sense of humor allowed him to see the good in people, and even helped him in his various dealings with members of the animal kingdom. For a time, there was a pack of wild dogs attacking the local sheep population as often as two or three times a week.

"Dad, the dogs are howling again," Pliny would whisper as he shook Willard awake.

"Grab your gun, boy," Willard would say as he reached for his boots and his Winchester.

Out the door they would charge, guns firing, to scare away the dogs. The dogs killed for fun, and at times the community would lose up to twenty head of sheep in a single evening.

Willard also raised prize-winning boar pigs. One of his champions had grown razor-sharp tusks of nearly ten inches in length. One day, the temperamental pig waited until Willard turned away, then hooked Willard's leg with his tusk and tore a huge gash down his leg.

Not to be bested by a boar, Willard jumped over the fence, grabbed an iron bar, and immediately applied some "emergency dental extraction" of the pig's tusks. Following the procedure, Willard hobbled into the house leaning on Pliny's shoulder, where medical help was summoned to stop the severe bleeding and to save his life.

But it was with a bull from the royal blood lines of England that was the real test, and where Willard met his match.

Willard Bean with one of his prize rams. The
Sacred Grove is in the background.

One day, Willard limped in from the hay fields and paused at the sheep pen at the side of the barn. Holding out his hand toward his prize ram, he snapped his fingers, beckoning the proud sire of the heard to come. Obediently the ram responded. Willard winced a little as he tried to bring his other arm up to grab the curled horn of his champion.

"Why can't the others be more like you?" Willard asked as he waited for the pain in his shoulder to subside. "You could teach the others around here an awful lot, you faithful one, you really could."

Willard grabbed the thick wool on the ram's neck and combed it with his fingers for a moment, and then painfully made his way across the front yard of the Smith home and in through the back door. The smell of fresh bread Rebecca had just retrieved from the oven filled his lungs and brought a smile to his face providing some needed balm for his bruised and broken body.

It had been over three weeks since he and the bull had squared off. The bull would soon be history, but would manage to leave his mark on the Mormon Cyclone. Willard looked at Rebecca fondly as she put a loaf of hot bread, butter, and honey in front of him and handed him a knife.

"I'm afraid I have met my match," Willard said. "That bull has rung all twelve of my bells and left me hanging from the lights. I think I will take my chances with the mobocrats and apostates. They're more my weight division."

Willard's mind raced back to his first mission call in the 1880s when he was assigned to protect and watch over the Presiding Bishopric and other General Authorities in their various travels. He was only a teenager then, but he was more than capable. Conditions in the Church at that time made it dangerous for many of the authorities to be in the open for fear of arrest or other danger. He loved protecting the Lord's leaders and guarding their safety, and he was good at it.[1] Rebecca's voice brought Willard to his present woes.

"Willard," sighed Rebecca as she turned her head with concern, "you're not as young as you used to be, and besides, Old Duke probably outweighed you ten to one. What do you expect?"

"I know, I know. But it's the challenge of the whole thing. Man was not meant to be in bondage to some old bull, and when he got filled with pride, I just had to bring some things to his remembrance."

"And look what it got you," Rebecca said, handing him a bowl of hot stew. "You're lucky to be alive. After all the times the Lord has saved you throughout your life, how would it look, both in heaven and here on earth, to finally meet your demise at the horns of an old bull? I hope you will do a little remembering yourself. You're over a half-century old, you know."

Willard knew she was right. He silently ached his way

---

[1] President Don B. Colton, Funeral Transcript of Willard W. Bean, in possession of the author.

through Rebecca's delicious meal and then retired to his writing desk to pen a letter to Bishop David A. Smith.

August 1, 1926

Dear Bishop Smith,

I note what you say about the bovine. It would appear that he got hold of some fight weed while at the other farm as he came back full of braggadocio with a chip on his shoulders. He came home Saturday evening. I greeted him almost affectionately and thought I would be kind to him by brushing the flies off when he showed his appreciations by diving at me. I sidestepped him and secured a piece of inch pipe near by and accepted his challenge. I met him in fair combat taking no undue advantage and, as I supposed, decisively defeated and conquered him. He retreated out into the pasture, but made an awful roar about not feeling altogether satisfied with his showing.

All evening and all day Sunday he was decidedly on the warpath. He wanted to fight everybody and everything. Monday morning we decided to put a brass ring in his nose and strap a heavy chain to his foot. Accordingly we let him out into the yard where I roped him and snubbed him to a tree, but our hired man being a little sympathetic suggested that we re-adjust the rope so it wouldn't choke him. I told him that we paid little attention to such things out west, but being cognizant of the bull's aristocratic lineage, I decided to show him the courtesy due his breeding, and acquiesced to the suggestion. The bull was an Ayrshire and registered under the name of Duke (Duke of Ayrshire), hence we naturally expected gentlemanly behavior on his part.

But quite to the contrary, when we began re-arranging the rope he got loose, and without provocation or extending the usual courtesies of the ring willfully attacked me, taking me unawares, knocked me down the first pass and proceeded to transgress every rule known to Queensbury ethics. Any competent referee would have disqualified him the first round for hitting while I was down. It began to look like I would have to take the count, but after he had bowled me out of bounds, just as my second, the hired man, diverted his attention which gave me a chance to regain my feet even though I was a bit groggy. After the usual rest I renewed the bout, this time taking the aggressive. I roped him again, snubbed him to a tree, strapped a chain to his foot, but feeling somewhat in distress, I held him down while the hired man cut a hole through his nose and rung him. Also we hung a small chain to his nose.

I was pretty well mussed up. Clothes all green where he had mashed me along the ground, face bruised and bleeding, leg and wrist lame and two slats [ribs] broken. Have been in adhesives and bandages since, but am fast getting back to normal. The bull became worse. He couldn't stand to see even a horse in the pasture, and would bellow and show fight every time anybody would come in sight of him. Needless to say we, as a final remedy, let the executioner have him who, in turn converted him into aristocratic bologna.

Of course, it would have made a better contest some 25 years ago when I was up in the art. But I never did qualify as a matador even though I have been to Mexico. I think my worst disappointment was that when it was all over and I looked around there was no movie machine in sight and not enough audience to give a merited applause. All wasted energy, and me a wreck.

But all joking aside—it might have been worse. Came at bad time of year when I should have been in the hay field. Bones have knitted and bruises about gone. Am around as usual and many things I can do but some things I can't do. But, work not suffering. Crops behind schedule and began to look discouraging until a fine rain came a few days ago which gave us cheer.

All well here.

Sincerely your brother,

Willard W. Bean[2]

---

[2] Letter to Bishop David A. Smith, Church Historians Office.

CHAPTER 7

The harsh winters of western New York were brutal long before the Beans arrived. November through March were often icy and dark and families ventured out of doors with much greater caution and planning than during the rest of the year. During many years on the Smith farm, the snow was so deep that a tunnel had to be dug from the house to the chicken coop in order to feed the fowl and gather the eggs. The tunnel lasted all winter until the first thaw.

The proof that spring had arrived was always in the voices of the children. Palmyra would sit quietly on the front steps of the Joseph Smith home as her younger brothers Pliny, Dawn, and Kelvin chased each other aimlessly around the trees in the front yard. It was late spring, and the ice of an unusually harsh winter was finally giving way to the warmth of the sun and its illuminating rays of light. It was at this time every year that Rebecca would prepare a picnic basket for the children and send them off to the protective maples and oaks and elms of the Sacred Grove. Palmyra waited anxiously as Rebecca put the last sandwich inside the basket and brought it to the front porch.

"All right, children, it's finally ready," Rebecca said with a smile as she handed Palmyra the picnic basket. "I hope you're hungry as a horse. Now you all scoot and have a fun time. Palmyra, you're the oldest. You be sure and take care of your brothers. Run along, now."

Palmyra loved this time of year, almost more than any other. Summer was right around the corner and that meant playing outside, fireflies, and a warm bed to snuggle into at night. There were no fireplaces in the upper rooms of the Smith home and heat was always a scarcity in the winter. Before going to bed she would carefully wrap in a towel a hot iron, or sometimes a rock that had been warming on the kitchen stove for hours. Those hot irons and rocks made going to bed bearable for the first 20 years of her life. But there was no need of a hot iron today. Spring had tenaciously leaped upon them.

"Pliny, don't you run so fast," yelled Palmyra. "Wait for Dawn and Kelvin."

"Well hurry up then and stop taking so long," answered Pliny. "You guys are so slow. I'm hungry. Come on."

Off to the west they ran, passing through the acres of wild daisies that surrounded the Smith farm that time of year. It was beautiful to watch as they laughed and danced their way, stopping only once at Hathaway Brook to negotiate their crossing and to throw some rocks. Then up the old dirt road they scampered toward the sacred little grove of trees. As they approached the seven-acre stand of timber, the wild daisies around the home gradually gave way to a colorful carpet of pink, purple, and white violets that covered the floor of the grove.

By the time Palmyra and the two younger boys arrived at the entrance to the grove everything was quiet. Pliny was standing speechless, a minor miracle, staring off into the luscious flowers and green foliage. Palmyra lowered the basket she was carrying to the ground and reached out for the hands of Dawn and Kelvin, who also stood in reverent awe. There was something very, very special about this place. Every time they came to this grove of trees, their laughter stopped, their yelling ceased, and their spirits warmed. There was no one there to make them be quiet, to restrain them, to silence them. It was as though the

Willard, Rebecca, Palmyra, and Pliny, in the daisies at the Smith Home.

world had stopped. They had been taught and they knew well the story of the First Vision. They knew what had happened in this little stand of trees a century before, and the image of that event rolled through their minds.

"Come, children," whispered Palmyra as she picked up the basket of food. "Let us go to our special place."

Silently they made their way through the grove until they reached a large sugar maple growing spaciously amidst the younger upstart saplings of beech and elm. Tradition had pointed to this spot as the place where the young boy prophet had knelt in prayer.

Several of the larger trees in the grove were old enough to have been there at the time of the First Vision. No one knew for sure if this was the exact place, but it didn't matter. What they did know was that something very special had happened here, something out of heaven. Every time they entered this little piece of forest it felt different from any other piece of forest anywhere.

The children ate their sandwiches and cookies and drank their milk as they whispered to each other. It was like this every year when they came for their picnic or whenever they visited the grove. Often the children were called upon to take visitors to the grove and invariably they were asked where it was that the prophet had knelt in prayer.

Palmyra, sitting with her picnic basket, at the entrance to the Sacred Grove.

In May of 1919 Charles F. Steele visited the grove with five-year-old Palmyra as his guide. He records in his diary the following:

A life-long hope was realized this morning when, in the company with adorable little Palmyra, tiny hostess of the old Smith homestead, I found myself nearing the Sacred Grove . . .

"*This is the Grove,*" *said Palmyra, simply, divining my desire to be undisturbed in my devotions. We entered together, soon reaching the heart of the wood.*

"*This is where little Joseph prayed,*" *said Palmyra softly, pointing to a particular tree which tradition says marks the spot where a child's faith moved the heavens and called to earth the Father and the Son.*

In silence I meditated and in overflowing gratitude my soul teemed with rejoicing unto the Most High......

"'*Palmyra, Palmyra, dear! Did you not hear the story of the Grove?'I cried.*

"*My only answer was the rustle of the leaves. The little child had gone.*"[1]

The children rested their heads back on the soft green fauna and purple violets that carpeted the grove and stared up into the dense tree tops. Palmyra felt the warmth of the sun melt across her face as the small shafts of light knifed their way through the leaves. Rushing through her mind came the happenings a century ago on this hallowed piece of ground.

Her parents had taught her that a young boy, about her age, had come into this grove of trees and prayed, wanting to know the truth about God and religion. The Bible said to ask for wisdom, and Joseph did. God said he would give wisdom, and He did.

It was not just an answer. It was an actual appearance, a visitation, a real and visual discussion with deity. Joseph not only heard with his own ears, but saw with his own eyes, the great God of the universe. He was not some invisible, gaseous mass of nothingness. He was a man, a glorified, immortal being of exquisite light and power. He was a God, worthy of worship. He was a Father, our Father, and one who loves His

---

1 *The Improvement Era,* "The Sacred Grove," 1920.

Palmyra playing on the fence line leading to the Sacred Grove.

children, just as fathers are supposed to. He talked with Joseph, and introduced him to His only begotten and most Beloved Son, the great Jehovah, the resurrected Lord and Savior of all mankind, Jesus Christ.

The two of them came in resplendent, immortal glory, on this very spot of earth, bursting the shackles of darkness and ignorance and answering once and for all the most pressing question of religion: "What is truth, and which church is right?"

Palmyra wiped the tears from her eyes as she pondered the truths restored in the Sacred Grove. Somewhere close by, maybe on this very spot, it had happened. She knew it had happened, and that truth would change her life forever. She knew, even more than she knew she lived, that these things really happened.

"Come children, it is time to go," Palmyra whispered.

"Mother will be worried. Let's pick some violets for Mama. You know how she loves them."[2]

Slowly and quietly they filled their hands with purple and pink as they meandered their way out of the south end of the grove. Eastward, in the distance, a beautiful white frame house beckoned them home.

"Last one home's a rotten egg!" bellowed Pliny as he darted down the well-worn path through the field.

"Oh yeah!" Dawn replied as he chased Pliny toward Hathaway Brook.

Palmyra took hold of Kelvin's hand and began to laugh as she pulled him faster than his little legs could run. They were back in the world again, and there was no more need to whisper.

Soon afterward, Willard stood at a makeshift podium in the Sacred Grove, speaking to Church leaders and missionaries. He concluded his talk by saying, "Brothers and Sisters, we have enjoyed a wonderful conference today and the spirit of the Lord touched our hearts and souls in a very real way. Some of that is because of what happened in this very special place many years ago, and also because of who we have with us today. We have been pleased to have Dr. James E. Talmage, of the Quorum of the Twelve, with us in this conference. It is a special honor for all of us to be in his presence.

"Following our closing hymn and prayer, our conference will be adjourned, until we hold the next one. For those of you staying with us overnight, Sister Bean has prepared a warm meal for you to enjoy before you retire for bed. Please make your way to the home as soon as possible following our closing prayer."

As usual, Rebecca had spent the better part of the day

---

[2] Palmyra Bean Packer Interview, August 29, 2006.

L to R: John Harris Taylor, Joseph Fielding Smith, Rudgar Clawson,
President Heber J. Grant, Augusta W. Grant, James E. Talmage,
B.H. Roberts, in the Sacred Grove, September 23, 1923..

cooking and preparing sleeping quarters for the many guests. Caring for guests and visitors was as constant as the sunrise. Each year brought more and more visitors. But this night, as the guests finished their meal and retired to their beds, there was one missing.

"I haven't noticed Dr. Talmage this evening," Rebecca remarked. "Do you suppose he is still in the grove?"

"I haven't seen him since our conference ended four hours ago," Willard said. "I will light a lantern and try to find him."

As Willard entered the grove, he heard the sound of footsteps. In moments, Dr. Talmage appeared.

"Forgive me, Dr. Talmage," Willard said. "I was afraid you might have gotten turned around in the grove and were unable to find your way out."

"No, Brother Bean. Everything is fine. I was just on my way out now."

Then, without any forewarning, Dr. Talmage commented, "Oh, the things I have seen and heard this day . . ."

The two men of God walked back to the house in quiet solitude, with Willard not wanting to interfere with the workings of heaven. Dr. Talmage sat down at the kitchen table with a bit of exhaustion.

He looked at Rebecca and said, "Sister Bean, could I trouble you for just a little bread and milk for supper? And Willard, can you get me a Bible and a Book of Mormon? I would like to read some passages of scripture."

Willard then asked, "I guess we'll read some of your experiences you had today in the *Deseret News*, won't we?"

"Brother Bean," answered Dr. Talmage with exactness. "When I tell the authorities what I have seen and heard this day, I'm sure they won't want to print it."

He then concluded, in almost a whisper, "My poor, poor people."[3]

Willard and Rebecca looked at each other in silent wonder, searching each other for some kind of meaning to what the apostle had just said, and hoping he would say more. But he did not. His experiences in the grove that day and evening remain locked in the vaults of heaven.

---

3 Rebecca Bean, Fireside Talk, 1964.

CHAPTER 8

Year after year Rebecca cooked and cleaned for hundreds of weary travelers. When all of the beds and floor space were taken in the home, the hayloft in the barn was soft and warm. Pliny and his brothers loved sleeping in the hay, and they were more than happy to give up their beds to guests and visitors.

Rebecca had no time for vacation or diversion from duty. If she was gone, who would take care of the visitors and the missionaries? Just once during her twenty-four year mission, did she travel with her children back to Utah to visit relatives. Her absence caused much indigestion and discomfort for the visitors who came while she was gone, for the bread Willard made always rose and fell like the setting sun.

Almost every afternoon or evening someone would arrive on the front porch of the Smith home and knock on the door. Rebecca would leave the kitchen in the rear of the home and answer the door. This day was no exception.

"Sister Bean, my name is Elder Crosby," the visitor said, thrusting his hand forward into hers, "and this is Elder Rasmussen, Elder Pearson, and Elder McKay. Behind them are Elders Smoot and Warner. We have finished our missions and are on our way back to Utah. Is it be possible to spend the evening here before catching our train tomorrow in Rochester? We promise not to be any burden."

"Please come in, Elders," welcomed Rebecca. "You are never a burden and you are welcome to stay as long as you would like.

Constant conferences brought many cars to the Joseph Smith farm.

Why don't you set your suitcases down and I will have one of my children take you out to the Sacred Grove for a while. You can spend some time there while I make your rooms ready."

The birthplace of Mormonism was a natural stopping place for anyone associated with the Church, and even some who weren't. General Authorities of the Church visited much more frequently now that the Church had returned to New York, and Eastern States missionary arrivals and releases all seemed to use the Joseph Smith Farm as the hub and crossroads of their journey. Missionary conferences were now as common as breakfast, for what better place to meet than in the Sacred Grove or on the slopes of the Hill Cumorah?

The six elders soon returned from their guided tour through the grove with young Palmyra. They found their bags had been taken upstairs to one of the four bedrooms.

"You'll find your rooms ready upstairs and as soon as you wash up, we'll have a warm meal ready for you," said Rebecca almost apologetically. "It's not much, but it's the best we have."

LDS missionary Thane Packer (Palmyra's future husband)
climbing a ladder to the hay loft sleeping quarters.

Little did the Elders know they would soon be eating a king's feast. The daily special was usually a plate full of hot mashed or boiled potatoes, beef and pork, a various array of freshly cooked vegetables, and all the hot bread, butter, and honey they could devour. Apple pie in a flood of rich cream finished them off.

Behind the Smith home, a little to the south near the chicken coop and ice house, stood the smoke house, where a side of beef or pork was continually hanging on the cure and being aged to perfection for the unexpected traveler. Mona Lisa, a very productive Holstein cow that was milked every morning by Pliny and evening by Palmyra, provided the rich cream that was churned into butter by the children.[1]

It was always a fantastic feast, but a kind compliment at the conclusion of the meal was the only pay Rebecca would ever receive.

---

[1] Palmyra Bean Packer interview, October 12, 2006.

"Sister Bean, did you know you're famous?" Elder McKay asked as the last spoonful of potatoes and gravy disappeared from his plate. "The word is out all over the mission: 'Don't leave to go home until you've had your last meal from Sister Bean at the Smith Farm.' And now I know why. It is simply the best meal I have had my entire mission. How do you do it? There are always so many who come, and we come so often."

Rebecca smiled modestly as she looked down for a long moment, lost in thought and silent dialogue with heaven.

"Elders, come with me into the next room for a few minutes. I have something I would like to share with you. Then you will understand the answer to your question."

The elders nestled into the soft chairs and sofa as Rebecca looked into their eyes with earnest.

"Please listen to what I am about to say," she said, beginning her story. "I don't share it very often, but I feel you should know what I am about to tell you. It was a hot summer day and we had a lot of visitors that day. It had been a hard day for me; I had a baby. He was just a year old and I had carried my baby around on my arm most of the day to get my work done. It was too warm and everything had gone against us and nighttime came and we had lunch for our visitors, and we had supper at night and I had put my children to bed and we had a very nice evening.

"Dr. Talmage was there with some missionaries and we had really had a wonderful evening talking together. So, they all seemed tired and I took them upstairs and showed them where they could sleep. When I came down I thought, 'Well, I will pick up a few things and make things easier for me in the morning.' But I was so weary and so tired that I was crying as I went and straightened things around in my house. Everybody was in bed and asleep but me. I looked at the clock and it was eleven o'clock and I can remember that I had said I had better call it a day. I went into my room and my husband was sound asleep and my baby also. It was peaceful and quiet. I got myself ready for bed. I said my prayers and I got into bed.

"I was crying on my pillow, and then this dream or vision came to me. I thought it was another day. It had been a wonderful morning. I had prepared breakfast for my visitors and my children were happily playing around and I had done my work and cared for the baby and he was contented and happy and then I prepared lunch and I called our visitors into lunch and we were all seated around the table, my little baby in his highchair and everything was just peaceful, wonderful and sweet.

"There was a knock at the front door and I went in and opened it and there was a very handsome young man standing there and I just took it for granted that he was just another missionary that had come to see us. I said, 'You're here just in time for lunch. Come with me.'

"As we walked through the little hall into the dining room, I noticed he laid some little pamphlets down at the end of the table there. We walked into the dining room and I introduced him around. Then I said, 'Now, you sit right here by Dr. Talmage and I'll set a plate for you.'

"I thought, of course, he was strange to all of us, and yet he and Dr. Talmage seemed so happy to see each other and they talked about such wonderful things while we were eating, some of them we could hardly understand, but the spirit that was there and the room was so peaceful and nice and everyone seemed so happy to be together. After the meal was over, Dr. Talmage said to the missionaries, 'Now let's go outside and just linger here and enjoy the spirit of this wonderful place, because we will soon have to leave.'

"I put my baby to bed and the other little ones went out to play and then I was alone with the young man. He thanked me for having him to dinner and told me how much it meant for him to be there. He told me he thought that the children were so sweet and well-trained and I felt so happy about that.

"Then we walked in the hall together and he said, 'I have far to go, so I must be on my way.' I turned from him for just a minute to pick up these little pamphlets he had laid on the table, and when I turned back to him it was the Savior who stood before me. He was in His glory and I could not tell you the love and the sweetness that He had in His face and in His eyes. Lovingly He laid His hands on my shoulders, and He looked down into my face with the kindest face that I had ever seen. Then He said to me, 'Sister Bean, this day hasn't been too hard for you has it?'

"I said, 'Oh no, I have been so happy with my work and everything has gone on so well.'

"He responded, 'I promise you, if you will go about your work everyday as you have done it this day, you will be equal to it. Now remember these missionaries represent me on this earth and all that you give unto them you give unto me.'

"I remember I was crying as we walked to the hall out onto the porch and He repeated the same thing. Then He started upward. The roof of the porch was no obstruction for Him to go through, nor for me to see through. He went upward and upward and upward. I wondered how I could see Him so far away. And then all at once He disappeared.

"Then I was crying on my pillow like I was when I went to bed. And I bear humble testimony to you that never again was there any frustration in my life. Never again did too many missionaries come that I couldn't find beds for them to sleep on or enough food to give them. The great love that I had for the missionaries even then became greater after what the Savior had said to me. How I wish that every missionary that went out in the world could feel that His love and His guidance are only a prayer away in preaching His gospel. Oh, how much they mean to Him."[2]

The missionaries sat in silence as they felt the magnitude of the message they had just heard from Sister Bean. They felt like they had felt earlier in the day when they had wandered through the Sacred Grove. It was the same spirit, undeniably from the portals of heaven, bearing witness of the reality and truth of the Son of God and his authorship of the restoration of the gospel through the Prophet Joseph Smith.

"Elders, you ask me how I can do this, and keep doing it day after day, and year after year," Rebecca said. "How can I not do it? I know who you are, and I know that all I do for you I do unto Him. Knowing that brings all the happiness into my life that I can handle."

The missionaries embraced Rebecca as they thanked her for this special moment, then quietly ascended the stairs for their last night in the mission field. Meanwhile, Rebecca returned to the remaining work in the kitchen in preparation for more unexpected visitors the following day.

[2] Rebecca P. Bean, Fireside Talk, 1964.

CHAPTER 9

Willard reached down into the bucket and grabbed a handful of black grease. He loved the feel of it on his chapped and often cracked and calloused hands. His hands were his tools both on the farm and in the boxing ring. He had learned to take care of them, and in return they would take care of him and anything else that needed to be done on the farm.

He coated the buggy's axle with a moderate layer of slick grease and then with his index finger applied a similar coat to the inside of the wheel hub. The open door of the barn provided more than enough light for Willard to do his work, and he smiled as he remembered his father always saying, "Work hard and fast, son. We're burning daylight."

Willard gritted his teeth as he hoisted the wheel up a few inches and carefully lifted it onto the axle. Grabbing a spoke of the wheel, he gave it a twirl and set the wheel spinning in a smooth and almost silent rotation. He watched as it turned free of friction or obstacle, and he wished the Church could someday spin and move as effortlessly as the wheel was doing.

The sunlight from the outside dimmed as a large shadow interrupted its flow through the doorway. Willard, with his back toward the door, sensed the intrusion and instinctively clenched his fists. He had been down this road before.

A man said, "Mr. Bean, I am the Reverend Abraham Silverstein from Charlotte, New York. I am honored to make your acquaintance."

"Reverend," Willard responded as he turned and began to walk toward the doorway. "I am honored to make your acquaintance also. Why don't we shake on it?"

Willard stretched forth his blackened and grease-caked right hand and grinned. The reverend returned the smile with a twinkle in his eye and held out his hand. "I'll go for that!"

"Just kidding, just kidding," Willard replied as they both responded with a friendly laugh. "Give me just a minute to clean up and I will be happy to grab that hand of yours."

Willard quickly poured some mineral spirits over his hands to dissolve the grease and grime and wiped them dry with a rag.

"Now, let's try that again, if you will," invited Willard as the two men exchanged a warm handshake. "I am sorry for the delay. If you don't mind my farmhand appearance, you are welcome to pull up one of our barnyard sofas and we'll chat a while."

Willard pointed to a bale of hay next to the buggy and quickly lifted another one down from the loft so the two of them could have a place to sit.

"I thank you for your kindness, Mr. Bean. I have been told of your friendly disposition and I am grateful for your willingness to spend some time with me. I presently am a minister in the Methodist Church and I understand you have frequented some of our congregations here in the Palmyra area."

"That is correct," Willard said. "After we had been here for a while we were invited to attend church services with your people and for the most part felt the hand of friendship, which I appreciate very much. I have always felt that just because people believe differently, it doesn't need to make them enemies."

"I agree with you, Mr. Bean. I totally agree. How else can one arrive at the truth, and when all is said and done, isn't that what we're really after? I think so."

Willard nodded. "But I have a question for you, if you don't mind. You say that you are a Methodist minister, and yet your name is Abraham Silverstein."

"Yes, that is correct," answered the guest.

"Unless I am mistaken, that name is rooted deeply in Biblical soil. It rings of Jerusalem and of Israel, through and through."

"Yes, my friend, you are right. I am a Jew, and yet I am a Christian. That is what has brought me here. I am fascinated and intrigued with the message of Mormonism. What little I know about it causes my mind to race back and forth between my ears. I hear the words of the ancient prophets in one ear and hear the message of Christ and His apostles in the other ear and they have battled each other all of my life.

"But when I study your beliefs, the battle stops, it comes together, it makes sense. I am hoping that you can tell me more? I am fascinated with your idea that there are prophets on the earth again and that angels are appearing again, just like in the Bible. I am intrigued with this Book of Mormon of yours. I want to know about it. Where did Joseph Smith get it? I must know for myself."

Willard listened intently to Reverend Silverstein. He felt the sincerity of his heart and his genuine pleadings to know the truth of all things. He admired any man who was not controlled by his own ignorance or intelligence.

"Reverend, you sound like Joseph Smith when he said, '*All I want is to get the simple, naked truth, and the whole truth.*'[1] If you will walk back to the house with me and drink some lemonade while I change my clothes and clean up a little, I would like to take you for a little ride in my buggy. As we do so, I would be honored to tell you about this book."

In a short time Willard and Reverend Silverstein were

---

[1] *Teachings of the Prophet Joseph Smith*, 372.

heading south on Stafford Road, exchanging pleasantries and getting further acquainted as they rode together.

"Reverend . . ." Willard began before being interrupted by his guest.

"Please, Willard, call me Abraham. If you persist in honoring me with Reverend then I must insist on calling you Elder, and I would be much happier if we talked as friends rather than ministers. And besides, I believe the name Abraham carries a whole lot more clout in the scriptures than does the word Reverend."

Both men laughed out loud as they nodded their approval of how to address each other. They continued to laugh until Willard noticed their destination in front of them. He pointed to a prominent yet mostly barren hill emerging before them. "There it is, Abraham."

Abraham leaned forward in the carriage to get a better view of what appeared to be the largest hill in the area. At the north end, near the base of the hill, a large elm tree rose majestically toward heaven, and on the west side there were a few trees not far from the top, but that was all. A smooth carpet of grass and wild flowers covered the remainder of the hill.

"Welcome to Cumorah," Willard said. "It doesn't look like much now, but in Joseph Smith's day it was really quite impressive. Early drawings show that the hill was completely covered with trees, as was most of this area. However, in the last hundred years forestry has given way to grazing as trees have been stripped from the land. It's my dream to restore this hill to its original landscape someday. It will take a lot of trees."

"So this is the hill where Joseph Smith found your gold Bible?"

"Yes, indeed. But he didn't exactly find it," Willard said, "and it really wasn't a Bible. Following the appearance of the Father and the Son to Joseph in the spring of 1820, three years

Hill Cumorah as it would have appeared to Abraham Silverstein.

transpired before he received further instruction from heaven. While praying in his room on September 21, 1823, an angel from the presence of God appeared to him and told him of an ancient record written on gold pages that was buried in the hill. Upon these pages were recorded God's dealings with the early inhabitants of this hemisphere, where they came from, and even the appearance and teachings of the resurrected Savior to them. The angel's name was Moroni, who was the last prophet to write in the book and who buried it in the hill around the year 421 A.D."

"Do you mean to tell me, Willard, that Jesus, the resurrected Christ, showed himself to the people on this hemisphere and actually taught them?"

"Why not?" Willard asked. "He is Lord over the whole earth and the Savior of all mankind. Don't the people here deserve to know about Him, just as much as the people in the Old World?"

"Willard, that is absolutely remarkable. In fact, it is not only remarkable, it is downright incredible. If what you say is true, the entire world needs to know about this. It is the greatest news since the coming of Christ. But Willard, how do you know it really happened? That is the question. And if it did happen, why doesn't the Bible mention it?"

"Those are good questions, and I will try and answer them for you," Willard said. "First of all, the Book of Mormon doesn't need the Bible to prove its validity. It can stand perfectly fine on its own. But, since you brought it up, let's see what it says about it."

"Surely you're not going to tell me the Bible mentions the Book of Mormon," Abraham said.

"Oh, it mentions it, but you need to remember that the great compiler of the record, Mormon, lived almost four hundred years after Christ. But the Savior and His prophets knew all about the people mentioned in the Book of Mormon. You just have to know what they are talking about."

"I'm all ears, giant ones," Abraham said. "Tell me more."

"My dear friend, consider the Lord's statement to his disciples in the Gospel of John. He says that there are other sheep that he has, not of the fold around Jerusalem, that He must visit, and that they will hear his voice. Who are those other sheep, and wouldn't they have kept a record if Christ visited them?"

"I am sure they would have. If the Savior appeared to me, I assure you, I would make a record of it."

Willard nodded. "And then there is the prophet Ezekiel, one of your blood brothers, who prophesies of two sticks, or records, to be joined together. Undoubtedly the stick of Judah that he mentions is the Bible. But what is the stick of Joseph? Where is this record of the descendents of Joseph?"

Abraham's jaw dropped a little as his piercing eyes seemed to look right through Willard. There were no words coming out of his mouth, but inside of him a mighty conversation ensued. Questions he had wrestled with for a lifetime were being answered. His spirit felt illuminated. Light and truth were chasing away centuries of confusion he had inherited with the rest of the world. "Are you telling me that the Book of Mormon is that stick of Joseph mentioned by Ezekiel?"

"You are a whole lot smarter than I am," Willard said. "You have been a student of religions all of your life, both Christian and non-Christian, Jew and gentile, but I don't see them giving answers to all of these questions that have tantalized the souls of men since the beginning of time. Think about it, and just be honest with yourself. But you need to know that what I have told you is true. The words I have said are the truest words that have ever been spoken to you. That which you have felt is the Holy Ghost testifying to you of the truth of the things we have talked about. The peace, the warmth, the light and the freedom from ignorance that you feel is of God. Remember the Savior's great counsel that the truth will make you free."

Abraham nodded his understanding and approval as he felt Willard's sincerity and conviction. He truly did feel peace in his heart every time Willard answered his questions. For the first time in his life the gospel seemed to be coming together.

"Can we walk up the hill, Willard? I would like very much to walk on this hill."

"Let's do it!"

Willard grabbed the steel rail on the front of the buggy and launched himself forward, turning a complete somersault with a half-twist in mid-air, landing squarely on both feet.

"My goodness," shouted a surprised Abraham. "Where did you learn to do that?"

"Oh, it's just a little bit of my younger days coming out of me. It keeps me young, and helps my joints stay loose."

"Well, please don't expect me to try it or I will lose my joints forever!"

Laughter again was a bond between the two men as Willard tethered his horse and buggy near the base of Cumorah. They had known each other for only a few hours, but it was as though they had been lifelong friends. The two men walked toward the western slope of the hill, veering a little northward to reduce the sharp ascent to the summit.

"Do you have any idea where the plates were buried on the hill?" Abraham asked.

"No one knows for sure," Willard answered. "Joseph mentioned in his history that the plates were buried on 'the west side of the hill, not far from the top, under a stone of considerable size.' He describes the stone as 'thick and rounded in the middle on the upper side, and thinner toward the edges, so that the middle part of it was visible above the ground, but the edge all around was covered with earth.'[2]

"Of course, there were trees all around in his day so the hill looked much different. I can show you where tradition has placed the spot, but it is purely supposition."

"I would like to see that, Willard, if you don't mind."

"Let's turn and head south, then, toward those few trees you see in the distance," Willard said as he pointed to the only trees on the west side of the hill.

Willard put his hand on Abraham's shoulder. "Be a little careful as you walk, Abraham. The hill still has many holes and trenches, dug over the years by zealous treasure seekers. After Joseph obtained the plates an engineering firm called The Rochester Company came and dug tunnels and trenches all over the hill, trying to find more gold. I have always thought it kind of strange that no one believed that Joseph Smith obtained a gold record, but there sure have been a lot of people who have dug around on this hill looking for gold!"

---

[2] *Joseph Smith History*, 1:51.

The two men continued their walk southward across the western slope of the hill. As they approached the trees, Willard stopped and looked around, trying to establish his bearings.

"After we arrived in Palmyra and were eventually able to walk on the hill without being threatened, I noticed a single rosebush growing in this area," Willard said. "I was told by some of the old timers here that the rosebush marked the spot where the plates were buried.[3] Somewhere, here amongst these trees, is where it is believed Joseph found the plates."

A photo taken in 1920 on the west side of the Hill Cumorah showing the reported site where the gold plates were buried.

Willard watched as Abraham slowly walked between the trees. For a moment he would stare at the ground, immersed in thought, and then raise his gaze to the vast and beautiful acres of trees and farmland that seemed to flow outward from this impressive hill.

"Is there anything more you can tell me, Willard? Is there more evidence or proof of this record that Joseph found?"

---

3 Rand H. Packer, *History of Four Mormon Landmarks in Western New York*, 22.

"Oh, not much Abraham," Willard responded. "I know that in 1873, when Edward Stevenson, one of our Church historians visited the hill, he was told that some of the sizable flat stones comprising the stone box that had contained the gold plates had been rolled down to the bottom of the hill and that people had seen them."[4]

Another 1920 photograph that shows the traditional
site where the gold plates were buried.

Willard added, "That is maybe nice to know, but it really doesn't make it true. Even if the plates were in our possession today, it still wouldn't prove anything. Moroni, the prophet who buried the plates, wrote in the book itself, 'I am the same who hideth up this record unto the Lord; the plates thereof are of no worth because of the commandments of the Lord. For he truly saith that no one shall have them to get gain; but the record thereof is of great worth.' The real proof of all of this is in the pudding."

"What do you mean, Willard? I'm not quite sure what you're trying to say."

4 Edward Stevenson, *Reminiscences of Joseph, the Prophet, and the Coming Forth of the Book of Mormon*, 28-29.

Willard smiled. "With the Bible, wouldn't you agree that it is the record that is important, not the scrolls it was written on? You preach at your pulpit every Sunday from the Bible. How do you know the Bible is true? You've never seen the scrolls from which it was translated. Nor have you seen the caves or the depositories they were stored in over the centuries, or talked with anyone who has. So, how do you know it is true?"

"Well," Abraham said, "I guess it is because I have read it and studied it and the Holy Spirit has told me in my heart that it is true. I just know that the Bible is the word of God."

"Exactly!" Willard exclaimed. "It is the same for me. That is how I know the Bible is true. If God has told you and me that the Bible is true, then don't you think He can tell you that the Book of Mormon is true? I know He will, if you will just read it and pray about it. I have done just that. I have read it and I have prayed about it. I know that the Book of Mormon is true, and that it is the Stick of Joseph that Ezekiel prophesied of to come forth in the latter days. I know it as much as I know I live. It is either true or false, Abraham. It shouldn't take a man of your stature and intellect very long to find out, if you really want to know."

Abraham remained silent for a long time. He had felt something as Willard had been talking about the Book of Mormon. It was a familiar feeling, one he had felt many times before as he read the Bible.

"Abraham, I could probably pile a lot of physical evidence right here in front of you, but that wouldn't make the book true. Even if we had the gold plates today and I could show them to you, it still wouldn't make the Book of Mormon true. The only way to know is to read it and to pray about it. That is why at the end of the book Moroni invites all readers to pray and receive their own answer as to its authenticity. But you must ask God, who is the author of all truth. I have a copy of the Book of

Mormon at my home. I will give it to you, friend to friend."

As the two men rode back to the Smith farm, Abraham asked many additional questions, and Willard answered them without hesitancy. Every question that Abraham could think of was met with the simplicity of the truth and light restored through Joseph Smith.

As they reached the farm, Abraham said, "Willard, during the summer while the minister in Rochester is on vacation, I have charge of his congregation. Will you come in a couple of weeks on a Sunday night and tell them what you have told me and let them ask you questions, as I have done? They need to know these things. Will you please come and occupy the pulpit in my church? It would mean a lot to me."

"You just say the word, Abraham, and I'll be there." [5]

---

5 *Willard Washington Bean Autobiography*, 3:36.

CHAPTER 10

The Methodist Church in Rochester had rarely been so full. For two weeks Abraham had worked overtime to invite his congregation and any others interested in learning more truth to come and enjoy a gospel discussion. Willard had been asked to speak for forty-five minutes and then to take thirty minutes to answer questions. He spoke eloquently, explaining the Joseph Smith story, his First Vision in the grove, Moroni's appearance and the coming forth of the Book of Mormon. He talked of John the Baptist, and Peter, James, and John restoring the priesthood of God back to the earth again following the apostasy in the early centuries. The congregation was respectful and listened intently.

Willard concluded, "Ladies and gentlemen, friends, and in a very real sense, my brothers and sisters, we have talked about some wonderful things tonight. I bear witness that the things I have said are true, and that Joseph Smith did see the Father and the Son and spoke to them. I know that he was called by them to be the prophet of the dispensation of the fullness of times. Now, if any of you have any questions, I will do my best to answer them for you."

"Mr. Bean, you say that Joseph Smith saw God and Jesus and that he spoke to them, but we all know that God is a spirit and has no body because that's what the Bible teaches. How could Joseph Smith see God if God doesn't have a body?"

"That is an excellent question and here is the answer. You are referring to the scripture John 4:24 where it says that God is a spirit. That has been translated incorrectly. Anyone who knows Greek will tell you that there are no indefinite articles in the Greek language. The verse should read God is spirit, just as in other places in the New Testament where it reads God is love, or God is light. You and I are spirit also, but it does not mean that we don't have a body. I see hundreds of bodies in this room tonight but it doesn't mean that you don't have a spirit. That verse was never intended to prove that God does not have a body."

Willard continued, "It is always much safer to look at all the scriptures together that talk about God's physical attributes, rather than just one. In Acts 7:55-57 Stephen looks into heaven and sees Jesus standing on the right hand of God. If Stephen saw them, then why couldn't Joseph Smith see them? The idea of God not having a body was never a doctrine taught by Jesus or any of His Apostles in the New Testament church. It gained popularity only after the third and fourth centuries when the different creeds began to appear."

"Mr. Bean, why do all you Mormons have so many wives? And, the talk around town is that you have two wives yourself."

"That is an interesting question, my friend. For many people polygamy is the only thing they have ever heard about The Church of Jesus Christ of Latter-day Saints. You ask a question about my personal life and I will answer it. I am the husband of one wife. That is the law of this land and it is the law of this Church, and we obey the law. Years ago I buried my first wife in the Salt Lake City cemetery and then later was married again to my second wife, Rebecca, whom I love very much. I would guess that in this room there are some who have had a similar experience.

"Secondly, it is true that in the early days of the Church there were some who were asked to live the law of plural marriage. If you know the Bible, which you all do, you will know that there were times when God not only permitted, but asked his people to live plural marriage. Two of the more notable ones are the prophets Abraham, from whence we get the Abrahamic Covenant, and Jacob, whose name was changed to Israel and who is also the father of the twelve tribes. And, since many of you in this room probably have a heritage through the children of Israel in one way or another, you ought to thank Abraham and Jacob for living this law, because if they hadn't, you probably wouldn't be here today."

Willard then held up his hand. "But polygamy is now a thing of the past. We believe that God commanded a prophet to have some members of the Church live it for a few years, and we believe that in 1890 he commanded us not to live it. Anyone living it today is excommunicated from the Church, and they would also be punished for being in violation of the laws of the land."

"I have heard, Mr. Bean, that all sorts of wild things go on in these temples of yours. What exactly are you doing in there?"

"Thank you for asking that very important question. Temples have been a part of God's work from the very beginning. You recall in the Old Testament the great temple of Solomon, and also the portable temple, called a tabernacle, in the days of Moses, which they used as they wandered in the wilderness for forty years. Then in the New Testament you remember Christ going to the temple and on one occasion driving the money changers out because they were desecrating His Father's house. So, it appears to me that God has always had a building called a temple wherein certain sacred ordinances were performed, separate from churches, synagogues, or places of worship. If I were looking for the Savior's Church today I would start by finding one that had temples also, because that is the way it has been from the beginning.

"I have had the privilege of serving over the years as an ordinance worker in the temple and I can tell you that everything that is done there is uplifting, beautiful, and for the salvation of God's children. In temples a man and a woman are married for time and for all eternity, and not just for this life only. Remember Peter, the apostle of old, who was given the keys of the kingdom, and the power to bind on earth and also to bind in heaven. Those keys have again been brought back to the earth and families can be bound together and not be separated at death. I really love the truth that a husband and wife and family can be together forever, even after they die.

"Now, I have a daughter, Phyllis, from my first marriage, who has been ill most of her life because of a bad heart. She passed away a short time ago and is now buried in the Palmyra cemetery. Let's just say she wasn't baptized or that she had never heard of Jesus Christ before, out of no fault of her own. She was a wonderful young lady. Would a loving God condemn her just because she had not the opportunity to hear about Christ or be baptized? I don't believe so. That is why the Bible teaches in First Peter 4:6 that the gospel is preached to spirits in the spirit world, and then they can be baptized by proxy here on earth, as taught in First Corinthians 15:29. Baptism for the dead, and other wonderful ordinances are performed in holy temples and have been since the very beginning."

"**Mr. Bean, that sounds so unbelievable to me. It is just too far-fetched to think that someone can be baptized for someone else after they die, by proxy as you say, and have it count.**"

"Well, you are welcome to believe whatever you want to believe. God allows all of us our agency. I am just telling you what He has said in the scriptures. But let me ask you a question. Do you believe in the Lord Jesus Christ? Do you believe that He came to earth, atoned for your sins as He suffered in Gethsemane and on the cross, and was resurrected so that you can be resurrected?"

The man nodded, and Willard said, "Then baptism for the dead should be easy for you to understand because the whole suffering of Jesus Christ for you is done by proxy. He stands in and suffers for you so you won't have to suffer for your sins, if you will repent. It is exactly the same principle. He does something for you that you can't do for yourself, and it counts. Otherwise, we are all in big trouble."

"Mr. Bean, you say this Joseph Smith is a prophet and that he received revelation and brought back the true church and more scripture. Everybody knows that the Bible is all of God's word and we can't add to it or take away from it."

"That is a great question. There are some that like to limit what God can say. I am not one of them. First, you must understand that we believe that Christ established and organized His church when he lived on the earth. You believe the same thing. Following His crucifixion there was an apostasy, prophesied of in the Bible, and that His Church, as He organized it, and the priesthood was lost. People changed doctrines to match their own interpretation, hence the many different Christian churches that we see today. Joseph Smith was the prophet God called to restore the true Church back to the earth, the same as it was in the days of Jesus. If I were looking for the true Church of Christ today, I would start by looking for one that had the same officers and organization. That is why Ephesians 2:19-20 is such an important scripture because it says that Christ's church is built on the foundation of apostles and prophets and that Jesus is the chief cornerstone. There were other officers, such as priests, deacons, elders, the seventy, high priests, and others. I would first look for a church that contained all of these officers.

As for having enough of God's word and not needing Him to speak to us anymore, I ask you this question. Do you have any children?"

"Yes, Mr. Bean, I have five children," the man said. "One lives in Canada, two are down in the Appalachians, one in the Shenandoah River Valley, and one lives clear out on the west coast."

"It sounds like you have a beautiful family," Willard said. "Do you ever talk with them, or send telegrams or letters, or visit them?"

"Every chance I get, especially now that the grandkids are making an entrance."

Willard nodded. "What if I were to tell you that you couldn't talk with them any more, or visit them, or communicate with them? From now on you would just have to make do with what you had said in the past."

The man shook his head. "Why those would be fightin' words, Mr. Bean. Don't you dare tell me that I can't speak to my children. If I want to speak to my children, I will speak to my children and nobody is going to stop me."

Willard smiled at him. "All right, I'm not going to stop you. It is what a father is supposed to do, to speak to his children. That is why you are their father. You continue to guide them and to help them and to speak to them.

"I think it would be wise on our part to allow our Heavenly Father the same courtesy. If he wants to speak to his children He will surely speak to them and there is no one here on earth that can keep Him from doing so. Our message to the world is that He has spoken, He is yet speaking, and that He will continue to speak to His children, because he loves them and we are His kids."

"If you don't mind Mr. Bean, I would like to go back to this idea of prophets. We all believe in the prophets of the Bible, and they wrote what God told them to write, and we now have it to read in his holy book. That's all we need and it solves all of our questions and problems."

"I know that is a common belief in all of Christendom and I respect that. Please know that I love the Bible, too, and I read and study it as much as you do. If the Bible is all we need, then why isn't it solving all of the confusion in the world, or even in Christianity?

"In Palmyra, the community where I live, there are four churches built on four corners at the Main Street crossroad. They all use the Bible and they all believe differently. Take a teaching like baptism, for example. There are some who believe that it must be done by immersion, and others do it by sprinkling or pouring. The Bible hasn't seemed to be able

Four Church Corners in Palmyra, New York,
Taken by Fellowcrafts Studios in 1920.

to solve that dilemma because people and ministers alike are interpreting the Bible as they so desire. Why so much diversity and difference in doctrine? Is that the way God wants it? I do not think so. He is not the author of confusion.

"Let us be reasonable and just a little bit wise. If the great Prophet Moses was going to be here in Rochester next Sunday and hold a meeting such as this, and answer questions about religion, would that be important to you? If the Apostle Peter, who led the Church after the Savior ascended to heaven, was to come and you really knew it was the Apostle Peter, would you go to that meeting? I would. I would walk from here to the Ozarks to hear him and would believe every word because he is God's prophet and he would know what the scriptures mean for sure. I want to know what God's prophet says about that verse of scripture, and not just someone's opinion or private interpretation.

"If ever there was a need for prophets in the world, it is now. God has always called and used prophets to guide his children. Why not now? I rejoice every day of my life and testify to you, that there are prophets again on the earth. I testify to you that angels have come from the presence of God and restored all of the rights and powers and authority and truth back to the earth again. The Church of Jesus Christ of Latter-day Saints is the same Church that Christ organized when He lived on the earth. I know as I live that there is a prophet today who can and does say, 'thus saith the Lord.' I know of a surety."

"**Mr. Bean, I have some further questions to ask, if you don't mind . . .**"

Willard held up his hands. "Ladies and gentlemen, I see that the time allotted me by your good Reverend Silverstein is all but gone, and then some. I apologize for going over my time. I think we should probably conclude this meeting, and then if you have further questions I will be happy to stay and discuss them with you. If that is all right with you, Reverend, I'll turn the time back to you."

Reverend Silverstein stood. "Thank you, Elder Bean, my dear friend. Brothers and sisters, I told you that this would be a good meeting, and it has been. I invite you to ponder the things you have heard tonight, and perhaps Elder Bean might consider coming again sometime in the future. I sincerely hope he will. Now, if George Simon will come forward and pray for us, our meeting will be over. George, your prayer, please."

It had been several days since Willard had met with Abraham's congregation. He had not stopped thinking about it. He had thanked the Lord many times since that evening for the opportunity afforded him to declare the message of the Restoration to so many people at the invitation of their minister.

Willard pulled a horseshoe out of the hot coals with the long-handled pliers and laid it flat upon the anvil. With a few powerful swings of the hammer he molded and shaped the shoe, which he would later in the day nail to Brownie's hoof. Keeping his

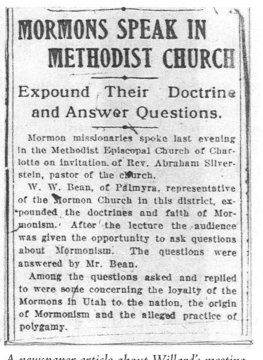

MORMONS SPEAK IN METHODIST CHURCH

Expound Their Doctrine and Answer Questions.

Mormon missionaries spoke last evening in the Methodist Episcopal Church of Charlotte on invitation of Rev. Abraham Silverstein, pastor of the church.

W. W. Bean, of Palmyra, representative of the Mormon Church in this district, expounded the doctrines and faith of Mormonism. After the lecture the audience was given the opportunity to ask questions about Mormonism. The questions were answered by Mr. Bean.

Among the questions asked and replied to were some concerning the loyalty of the Mormons in Utah to the nation, the origin of Mormonism and the alleged practice of polygamy.

A newspaper article about Willard's meeting with Abraham Silverstein's congregation.

farm horses in shoes was harder than keeping his children in shoes. He smiled as he thought about nailing some iron soles to the bottom of his children's feet. Not a bad idea, unless of course, they were planning on going swimming.

His mind soon went back to the evening he had spent at Abraham's pulpit. Things were changing. People were becoming more tolerant and open, and Willard could see the hand of the Lord at work. It would just take time.

Willard thrust the horseshoe into the bucket of cold water, the steam rising to his face as the hot iron sizzled into an enduring shape.

"We are all horseshoes," Willard thought, "forged and beaten and shaped by the Master's hand into something worthwhile. It takes time and it is hard, but remarkable we will become as the fire and the pounding and steam secures a shoe that will walk forever in His footsteps."

A few moments later he noticed a familiar shadow appear again in the doorway of his barn.

"Willard, I thought I would find you out here," Abraham said. "It is good to see you again."

"My good fellow, you brighten my day," Willard answered. "That bale of hay has your name all over it, and it's more comfortable than a lot of pews I have sat upon over the years. Sit down, sit down."

"I came to thank you for coming and speaking to my congregation last week."

"It was my pleasure, Abraham. I don't think that I did any damage. No one has asked me for a baptism interview."

Abraham frowned slightly. "Actually, I met yesterday with the Rochester Ministerial Association. They have revoked my certificate and taken away my ministry. I no longer have a congregation."

Willard was nearly speechless. "They did that just because

you invited me to speak to your congregation? How can they do that?"

"Oh, they can do it, and they have."

"I am so sorry, Abraham. I would never have come had I known. You have got to understand that."

'I know, I know. Remember, that it was I who asked you to come. It's a shame we can't just all learn from each other. Why are we so afraid of someone else's viewpoint?"

"Fear of learning truth seems to hold us all hostage, does it not?" Willard asked sadly.

"I don't suppose your church has a congregation that needs a minister, does it?" Abraham said with a little laugh. "I come pretty cheap. Are you sure you don't have a paid ministry?"

"Oh, I'm sure of that, Abraham. I would be a rich man if we did."

"You know what's funny? I have spent more than twenty years preaching only half the gospel, and now that I have discovered the full gospel, I have no one to preach to."

"Abraham, I am just without words, I don't know what to say, or what to do."

"There is nothing you can do, or should do," Abraham said. "You have given me so much to think about and to pray about. I thank you from the depths of my heart for the added light and understanding you have shared with me. I want you to know that I will never be the same. I hope you understand how believable your message is. In all of my years in the ministry, I have never heard the gospel explained so plainly and beautifully as you have explained it. I am in your debt forever."

"It is I that am in debt to you, Abraham. I believe that our friendship is most pleasing to God. We are two men, brothers and sons of God, talking religion without clubs in our hands. All we want to know is the truth and to do His will. We don't have to be angry and we don't have to fight for our position.

We just can share what we know, learn some things from each other, and find the truth, wherever it is. Surely He smiles upon both of us."

They embraced and bid farewell to each other. Willard stood for a long time at the door of the barn as Abraham walked briskly up the road until he vanished from sight. Willard slowly walked back into the barn and quietly approached the bale of hay where Abraham had been sitting. He stood there a long time as he pondered the sad news he had just heard. Reverently, and with rare emotion, Willard dropped to one knee and bowed his head in behalf of his friend.

"Dear Father, wilt thou bless this good man. Thou knowest the things that have happened and the injustice that has been done to him, all because he allowed me to share thy message with his congregation. Wilt thou remember him, dear Father. He is one of thy choice sons who desires only to know the truth. Please grant unto him the solicitations of his heart that he might come to know the truths thou hast restored. Remember, dear Father, his kindness to us, his willingness to look beyond the fences of bigotry and to recognize the goodness that abounds in all people who . . ."

Willard wasn't sure how long he had been on his knees, but it was long enough for his tears to moisten a path across his dust-covered cheeks. He solemnly arose and turned to face the task at hand. Slowly he reached down into an old wooden box leaning against the anvil and firmly grabbed a new horseshoe yet to be fitted.

"Come, let me pound you into something," Willard whispered.

He pumped the bellows several times as the sparks chased through the air above the forge. Securing the new horseshoe in the grasp of the long-handled pliers, he thrust it deeply into the glowing coals and waited with hammer in hand.

Note: Willard Bean's friendship and experiences with Reverend Abraham Silverstein are a matter of record as written in the *Willard W. Bean Autobiography.*

Following this experience Reverend Silverstein moved with his wife, his mother-in-law, and their three children to Binghampton, New York, where he became involved in a small printing business. There he wrote and co-published with another Jewish minister a small periodical called *The Redeemed Hebrew.*

The letter that is contained on the following two pages is a response from the First Presidency to Willard's report of his dealings with Reverend Silverstein.

The First Presidency
of the
Church of Jesus Christ
of
Latter-day Saints.

47 E SOUTH TEMPLE ST.

Salt Lake City, Utah

April 5th, 1921,

Elder W. W. Bean,
Palmyra,
New York.

Dear Brother:

        We have received and read your letter of March 30th,
with very much interest. We will certainly be glad to give
Rev. Abraham Silverstein proper entertainment when he calls at
our office.   There are a few preachers who would jeopardize
their jobs by publishing articles for elders of the Latter-day
Saints, and we notice this gentleman seems to have some
independence as a result of having something else to do. We
are always glad to hear of our elders having good friends in
the various locations where they are operating.

        Glad to note that you are well and that the spring
work is beginning to open up. It is interesting to know the
success you have had in raising lambs, although at the present
prices of wool we apprehend the results from the standpoint of
finances would not be very profitable.

        We note the little opposition the women have given
you but that, as usual, in such cases, it has reacted for the
benefit of the cause.

        It is most gratifying and surprising to note the
treatment that the Presbyterian minister is giving you, especially
since it seems to be the result of his having written to Salt
Lake for information respecting the "Mormons".   It is so seldom
that correct first hand information goes out to ministers in the
world. It all goes to show that you have been able to show your
friends in a dignified and proper way, some of the truths of
"Mormonism". We hope the friend of whom you speak as having
been useful to you there will be able to accomplish some good
at Syracuse.

        We rejoice in the blessing of the Lord to the
organist and Sunday School teacher who lost her voice and
had it restored to her through the administrations of his servants,
and her faith in the power of God and in the Priesthood. The

*A letter from President Heber J. Grant and his counselors in the
First Presidency in 1921 to Willard Bean concerning Abraham
Silverstein's possible visit to Church headquarters in Salt Lake City.*

- 2 -

Elder W. W. Bean.   April 5, 1921.

signs do follow the believers in this day the same as they did
in the days when our Savior was upon the earth.

       We rejoice in the spirit of your letter and in the
interest you are taking in the work of the Lord. We pray our
Father in Heaven that He will continue to pour out his Holy
Spirit in rich abundance upon you, that you may have wisdom and
knowledge given you from time to time that will enable you to
cope with every situation and surmount every difficulty.

       Ever praying the Lord to bless you in your labors,
and with our very best wishes, we are,

              Affectionately your brethren,

              [signature]

              Charles W. Penrose

              [signature]
                   First Presidency.

CHAPTER 11

It was always a thrill for Willard to climb the slopes of the Hill Cumorah and to look out over the vast Fingerlakes district of western New York. He would often visualize the great events that had taken place in the Book of Mormon that culminated at this hill.

Ancient nations had become extinct because of their failure to follow the God of the universe who had set aside and preserved this land for His righteous purposes. Great battles had been fought as the forces of good and evil waged their continual war.

Often Willard would ask himself, "If you could talk to me Cumorah, what would you tell me? What would you have me know? What great secrets could you bring forth to help this hungry and hellish world?"

At times he would sit upon the hill and read in the Book of Mormon about the Lord's great efforts to bless and save His children. The book was a solid foundation of truth to him, a companion to the sacred and Holy Bible. For centuries it had remained buried in this hill, waiting for Joseph Smith to uncover it.

At times like these, like the constant waves of the sea surging upon the shore, Willard felt the strong urgings of the Spirit to obtain the hill for the Church. He knew the Lord had further plans for this hill and that it was imperative that he do all he could to obtain full possession of Cumorah.

Willard had faith that the way would somehow open up for this to happen. The opportunity was set in motion one day when he was asked to visit the office of Pliny T. Sexton, the principal owner of the Hill Cumorah. It had been a while since he had talked with Mr. Sexton, and he was not sure why the banker had summoned him to his office.

Mr. Sexton was a kind and generous man, wearing his Quaker heritage with boldness. His pleasant demeanor was surpassed only by his ability to make money, and his large bank complex spoke well of his abilities as a financier.

Willard entered the bank and walked through a short hallway past the tellers. The hallway opened up into a very impressive fire-proofed office area where Willard was greeted properly by a well-dressed receptionist.

"Good day to you, sir," the woman said. "May I help you?"

"Yes, thank you." Willard responded. "I am here to see Mr. Sexton. I have an appointment with him."

"Ah yes, Mr. Bean. I am Harriett Sexton. He is expecting you. Come right in and I will show you to his office."

Willard followed Harriett, who was Pliny's wife and vice president of the bank, a short distance to a large door. She knocked quietly, then opened the door slightly. "Mr. Bean is here to see you," she said.

"Thank you, Harriett. Please have him come in."

She motioned to Willard, and he stepped through the door.

"Willard, my good man!" Mr. Sexton said as Willard walked into the room. "It is so good to see you again. It has been too long, way too long."

"I agree," Willard said. "I have been negligent, I must say, in my duties to be neighborly."

"Nonsense!" Mr. Sexton bellowed. "You're just busy like the rest of us."

Willard had liked Mr. Sexton from the very first day he had met him. He was a kind and generous man on many occasions, but it never interfered with his tough and rigorous approach to business deals and acquiring wealth. Over the years he had accumulated nearly fifty properties and owned a quarter of the land in the city of Palmyra. He was a self-made millionaire and Willard admired that.

There was never any beating around the bush with Mr. Sexton, and Willard always knew exactly where he stood. The man was now more than eighty years old, and his full beard and mustache, white as the mountain snow, was groomed to perfection. His appearance reminded Willard of the Confederate General, Robert E. Lee. He was dignified, honorable, and filled with confidence and assurance.

"Tell me, Willard, how is the preaching going and how is that bandstand working out for your pulpit? Are you making any converts?"

"The bandstand is great and everything is going quite well, actually. Much of that we owe to you and your kindness in letting us use your property. We are forever in your debt."

"I learned long ago that it is always nicer being on the receiving end of indebtedness," Mr. Sexton said. "It's much more profitable. Maybe someday I will be in your debt and then we'll call it even."

Willard smiled. "You drive a hard bargain, sir, but I shall try to be equal to it."

"I want to show you something, Willard, that I think you will be very interested in seeing. It is one of my most prized possessions."

Like a child on Christmas morning, Mr. Sexton rose from behind his desk and hurried to a large safe bolted to the inside wall of his office. With precision Sexton turned two separate dials in rapid sequence and then inserted a key from his

*The property and park next to Pliny Sexton's bank which
he allowed Willard to use for street meetings.*

pocket. Willard heard the muffled click of metal on metal as
Sexton pushed the large lever downward, opened the door, and
retrieved a small grey box. He handed it to Willard and said,
"Have a look at this and tell me what you think."

Willard lifted the outer lid upward until the contents were
visible. Willard's eyes immediately danced with excitement.

"Mr. Sexton, where on earth did you get this?"

"I knew you would like it. It's an unbound printer's copy
of the first edition of your Book of Mormon. I obtained it
from John H. Gilbert himself, the typesetter of the book at the
Grandin Press. There was a time when he was deeply indebted
to me and past due on many payments. To erase his debt, I took
this off his hands. The book is a treasure, a real treasure."

"This is a rare item indeed," Willard said, "and absolutely
priceless."

Willard brought the pages up close to his face so he could
examine them closely and smell their antiquity. The pages
were beginning to curl a little on the edges, since there was no
binding to keep them pressed to each other. There was a little

discoloration on some of the pages due to the moisture and temperature making their mark over the years.

But it was the smell that Willard loved. It was kind of a dry and dusty smell, a musty combination of paper, wood and ink all rolled up into something archival and historical and spiritual. As he held it in his hands he could almost hear the voices of Emma Smith, Oliver Cowdery and Martin Harris, all of whom served as scribe for the Prophet Joseph as he translated from the plates of gold. He remembered Joseph's powerful witness and testimony of the translation process:

"I did translate the Book of Mormon by the gift and power of God and it is before the world, and all the powers of earth and hell can never rob me of the honor of it." [1]

Willard finally placed the pages back in the box. "Mr. Sexton, this has been a special day for me. I thank you so very much for allowing me to hold in my hands this relic of the history of our Church. I was wondering if you have ever actually read the Book of Mormon?"

"Oh, goodness no. I don't have much time for reading anymore. Besides, I am a Quaker, you know, and any reading I do is confined to God's holy word."

"I understand," Willard said, "but I feel my indebtedness to you and I would like to pay some of it off."

"I am not sure I know where you are going with this. It sounds to me as if you are ready to bargain."

"I am in no position to bargain for anything nor do I have a desire to do so," Willard said. "But I do have an observation."

"And what is that?" Mr. Sexton asked.

"You have just shown me a priceless printer's copy of the first edition of the Book of Mormon of which I will never forget. It would bring a pretty penny on the auction block. But what if I

---

1 *Larry E. Dahl and Donald Q. Cannon, "The Teachings of Joseph Smith," p. 92.*

Pliny T. Sexton is shown holding John H. Gilbert's
unbound printer's copy of the Book of Mormon.

told you that the words of the book, that printed ink on paper, if read and accepted, would bring a return on your investment more than a thousand fold in real wealth?"

Willard then continued, "You're a man that knows investment. Have you ever owned any property that has returned that kind of dividends? I think not. In the eternal scheme of things, I do know that all investments are not of equal value. Some things are just more important than other things, and that ought to be a prime consideration of any investment."

Mr. Sexton pondered for a few seconds the words that Willard had just spoken. "Willard, you surprise me a little. I judge you to be somewhat wiser than I had originally thought. I shall make note of our conversation."

Willard smiled as he said, "Maybe in my case it is just common 'horse sense,' though I would someday enjoy being classified with those who are considered to be wise."

"Well, enough of that," Mr. Sexton said. "Let's talk about some other things, shall we? How is that hill of yours doing that I still own most of?"

Willard pointed to the printer's copy on the desk, "you mean the hill where the Book of Mormon came from."

"Yes, that hill. Cumorah, I think you call it."

"Again, we find ourselves deeply indebted to you. Your kindness has allowed us to traverse your property so that we might enjoy the ninety-seven acres we bought from Mr. Inglis several months ago. On behalf of the Church I thank you for your gesture of friendship."

"I continue to be reminded of your indebtedness to me. I know a way you can remove your debt to me, Mr. Bean. A few years ago I offered Cumorah to you for $100,000.[2] That offer still stands, not a penny more. If you will take that hill off my hands for that same amount, we will call things even."

Willard couldn't help but smile. He said, "When you made that previous offer to us, I was shocked, and jokingly accused you of giving ear to the anti-Mormon claims of the tremendous wealth of the Church. Today, I am not shocked, but I am amused."

"Why are you amused?" Mr. Sexton asked.

"Land prices have risen steadily in the last few years, yet you are asking the same price as you did then," Willard said. "It only leads me to believe that it was terribly overpriced then and it is still overpriced today."

Sexton nodded a little as he acknowledged Willard's analysis of the offer.

"Let's be honest with each other," Mr. Sexton said. "We both know how valuable and important that hill is to your people. It

_____

2 In 1919, Sexton offered to sell his portion of the Hill Cumorah for $100,000. Details can be found in Cameron J. Packer's BYU Master's Thesis, *A Study of the Hill Cumorah*, p. 77.

is worth a king's ransom to you, you know that. Surely my offer is worth every penny to your Church."

"The position of the Church has not changed," Willard said. "We were unable to pay that kind of money then, and we are unable to pay that kind of money now. We have existed very happily the last one hundred years without the hill and there is no reason why we can't continue to do so. That hill belonged to God long before it ever belonged to you, and Moroni walked upon that hill before I ever did. I do believe, however, that we are both at God's mercy on this issue and that whatever happens will be according to His mind and will."

Both men looked at each other, neither one backing down. Mr. Sexton sternly glared at Willard for several seconds before saying, "Willard, I like you a lot. There is no doubt that your church has sent the right man out here. It is too bad we did not strike up an acquaintance in our earlier years. We would have made a very successful and wealthy team, you and I."

Willard quickly rose from his chair and stepped toward the center of the room. Without warning, he did a backward somersault, landing squarely on his feet with his hands openly gestured. "I am still in my early fifties, Mr. Sexton. We still have time."

Both men roared with laughter as they came together in a firm handshake and almost an embrace.

"We will see what the future holds, Mr. Bean, shall we not? In the meantime, enjoy the hill I keep trying to sell you."

The two friends parted company as Willard walked out of Mr. Sexton's office into the sunshine of Palmyra's Main Street. Heading east across William Street he looked back toward the park where his street meetings had found a home, thanks to the wealthy banker. Walking further east along Exchange Row, he looked through the windows of what used to be the Grandin Press Building, where the Book of Mormon was printed.

"Some day, perhaps," whispered Willard to himself, "we will acquire this special place also. The Lord will provide."

Months had passed since Willard and Mr. Sexton had enjoyed their bout concerning the sale of the Hill Cumorah. The winter had been harsh, as usual, but the spring planting had gone well and the hot and humid summer months made Willard almost long for winter again.

Willard came in through the back door of the house, tired and sweaty. Rebecca was waiting inside, knowing it was Saturday and that they would travel to Palmyra that evening for their customary street meeting.

"Willard, there's some fresh lemonade in the ice box," she called from the adjoining room. "It's been on ice all day."

Willard smiled as he walked toward the ice box. Hearing her voice reminded him, again, of how grateful he was for a woman that was his equal, and more so. She met his every need and most often worked harder than he did.

A tall glass was chilled and placed beside the pitcher of lemonade in the ice box. Willard grabbed one in each hand, closed the door with his elbow, sat down at the table and began pouring.

"Ahh," Willard sighed after devouring his entire drink without taking a breath. "My dear, why don't we open up a lemonade stand here on Stafford Road for the weary travelers? You would become famous, we would become wealthy, and everyone would remain sober."

As Willard poured himself another glass, Rebecca laughed and said, "You could be my squasher, and jump around on the lemons all day long."

"Oh, I almost forgot," she then added. "Did you hear about old Mr. Sexton?"

Willard's fatigue vanished. "What has happened?"

*Willard, Rebecca, and Lillian Wood in the room where the
Book of Mormon was first printed in the Grandin Press
Building, long before it was it was obtained by the Church.
Willard is holding a first edition of the Book of Mormon.*

"The Morgans came by this morning and said they had
been to town. They heard he is very ill and not expected to live
much longer."

"We shall stop and pay him a visit this evening, prior to our
street meeting," Willard suggested. "I must talk with him."

As Willard and Rebecca approached the National Bank
of Palmyra, the upstairs portion having been made his living
quarters, Willard could already see some of the town regulars
beginning to gather in the park for their weekly doctrinal
discussions. Willard knocked boldly on the door to the bank.
The door opened slightly.

"Yes, may I help you?" asked a uniformed nurse.

"We are Willard and Rebecca Bean, and we were hoping to see Mr. Sexton."

"He is not up to it, and visitors are not allowed under any circumstances," the nurse said. "He is doing very poorly and is totally bedridden. But I will tell him that you have called."

"Ma'am," Willard quickly said as the front door started to close. "If you will open his window in his bedroom upstairs so he can hear what I have to say, it will bring some comfort to him. Please mention that to him. Please!"

Willard thought he saw the nurse give a nod of confirmation, but he wasn't sure.

"Now, he will have to listen to me, like it or not," Willard told his wife as he began to rehearse in his mind a fitting sermon to help his friend. Willard began to coax the crowd closer to the bank as Rebecca's angelic soprano voice sang, "Nearer My God To Thee."

Charlie Collins, the first convert baptism in Palmyra, accompanied her on his violin.

When Rebecca concluded the song, Willard stepped forward and said, "Ladies and gentlemen, tonight and in the future I will give my addresses from this position near the bank of Mr. Sexton. As you know, he lies very ill at this time and perhaps a few of my words will be of interest and comfort to him. He has been a friend to us all, and we pray for him and wish him Godspeed."

Willard paused a moment and quickly stole a glance at the top floor of the bank as he heard the opening of a window above him. The nurse sternly nodded her head at him, then quickly turned away as he acknowledged, in return, her good efforts.

Willard continued, "This evening, I would like to talk about a question that has puzzled the souls of men from the very beginning. The question is, 'What happens to us when we die and leave our mortal existence here on earth?'

Sexton's home, office, and bank complex in Palmyra, New York.

"All of us, no doubt, have thought about this and have had friends and loved ones who have moved on to the eternities ahead. Death will happen to all of us and is part of the plan of our Father in Heaven. But where do we go, and what can we expect?"

Willard noticed that the crowd was particularly somber tonight and seemed attentive and interested to learn. He knew the Bible and the Book of Mormon thoroughly, and could probably quote more scripture than anyone else in the entire Church,[3] or any minister of any faith.

"The Book of Mormon tells us that anciently, on this continent, a prophet by the name of Alma had a son named Corianton, who was concerned about death and the resurrection," Willard taught them. "Like any good father,

---

3 "Willard Bean, Palmyra's Fighting Parson," *Ensign*, June 1985.

Alma taught his son. But, where did Alma get this knowledge? He says that it was made known to him by an angel from the presence of God. That, I think, is a pretty good reference. Let me read to you what the angel taught Alma and what Alma taught his son, Corianton. It is found in the Book of Alma in the Book of Mormon, chapter forty, starting with verse eleven. It reads, "Now concerning the state of the soul between death and the resurrection—Behold, it has been made known unto me by an angel . . ."

Willard's bull-moose voice reverberated through the night air so that everyone, especially his friend laying next to an open window above, could hear and understand. For the next several weeks, Willard preached from the same spot. He noticed the window was always open upon his arrival, as though his friend had been waiting all week for his message.

On one such night in early August, Willard was heavy into his sermon. Suddenly, a man toward the front of the crowd began to yell, "I see the light, I see the light!"

"I see it, too," yelled another.

Willard smiled, as it was not his desire to turn the meeting into a revival. He paused and looked behind him and then he saw the light, too. A large circle of light was moving recklessly all over the front of the building as the people seemed hushed by this miracle.

It took Willard but a moment as he followed the trail of the light that seemed to beam from across the street, having its origin from his old Graham-Page touring car where his young son, Pliny, was playing in the front seat.

"Pliny," yelled Willard loudly, but with love. "Pliny, turn the spotlight off. Thank you, son, now please leave it off now."[4]

All of the congregation had a good laugh and Willard

---

4 Vicki Bean Topliff, *The Life Story of Alvin Pliny Bean*, 116.

Willard's Graham-Page touring car in front of the Martin Harris farm.

continued on with a smile, without the help of any man-made miracles. When he had finished his street meeting, he gathered up his scriptures and a few pamphlets that had not been taken by the crowd and looked for Rebecca. She was standing next to the door of the bank and Willard could see that his wife and Mr. Sexton's nurse were in heavy conversation. Willard made his way toward the bank door.

"Oh, Mr. Bean," clamored the usually sullen nurse. "I was just telling your wife what a wonderful thing it has been to hear your preaching every Saturday evening. Mr. Sexton has listened to every one of your sermons and asks me every day if it was time for your next one. He has me open his window hours before so he would not miss it. He told me just tonight how you made the gospel so easy to understand and that he had never heard such a clear interpretation of the scriptures."[5]

5 *Bean Autobiography,* 2:34.

"I am so happy that he has been able to hear. I have spoken as loudly as I could because I know he does not hear well."

"You have come through loud and clear," the nurse said, "and it has been most helpful to him."

"Please let Mr. Sexton know that he is in our prayers and that I would enjoy the opportunity to speak to him as soon as he is well enough."

"I'll do that, Mr. Bean, and I will be sure to have his window open again next Saturday."

Willard and Rebecca walked together across the street to where Pliny was waiting anxiously in the car, stopping momentarily here and there, as people would shake their hands or thank them for the music and religious discussion. Instead of fists, an open hand was more common now, and vicious threats were giving way to words of gratitude.

"I have a feeling that our time with Mr. Sexton is past, and we will not see him again," Willard told his wife. "If he is gone, I doubt that we will ever obtain all of Cumorah."

"You have done all you can, dear," Rebecca said. "All we can do, is all we can do. Perhaps it is time to stand aside and let the Lord take it from here. He's pretty good on His own, you know."

Willard smiled approvingly at the humble and loving words of his faithful companion. It was good for him to be reminded that this was the Lord's work and no one else's, and that the great God in heaven was surely capable of performing His own work.

Pliny Titus Sexton died on September 5, 1924. He was eighty-four years old.

CHAPTER 12

The void left in Willard's life by Mr. Sexton's death was hard to fill. Friends did not come easily, especially ones of Mr. Sexton's prestige and caliber. But Willard seemed to have a gift that those around him always ended up liking him. Perhaps it was his ring savvy, or his sense of humor, or possibly his accepting nature. Whatever it was, he caused hateful hearts to change.

Willard and Rebecca had been invited by his blacksmith friend Simmons to attend Palmyra's annual Odd Fellows picnic and field day, but they were unsure about it.

"Simmons, thank you very much for the invitation, but I'm not sure that it would be a good idea for us to come," Willard told his friend. "I don't think we would receive a very warm reception."

"Willard, you'll be sitting at our table, and my wife and I will see to it that you are respected. A man's religion is his own business and it shouldn't make a gnat's difference on whether you like someone or not."

Simmons was a fine blacksmith and Willard had done business with him since first arriving in Palmyra. He was Willard's kind of man, and he wished the whole world had the common sense and wisdom of this iron beater.

"We'll come then," Willard said. "We really do enjoy these kinds of things. If it gets uncomfortable, we'll just kind of disappear. We don't want to cause trouble."

As Willard and Rebecca arrived, two of the Macedon lodges were getting ready for their baseball competition, but the umpire had not shown up. They asked Willard to substitute until he arrived, so he umpired and finished the game without any arguments.

As the relay races began, they put the starting gun in Willard's hand to make sure that everyone started moving at the same time. The jumping contests needed judging, so Willard did that. It was a good day for the Beans, or so they thought.

The following Tuesday at the lodge meeting, a riot nearly broke out. "Our citizens are up in arms," said a group representative, "because of the debauchery of our picnic and field day activities last Saturday. We and our families were outrageously disgraced and humiliated by being compelled to mingle with a Mormon polygamist and his family, who came without being invited."

Cheers and jeers went up throughout the lodge until the Baptist minister rose to take the floor. To his credit, this fine man faced the angry crowd and said, "I assure you that Mr. Bean is not a polygamist. He comes to our services periodically, and I personally wish he would come more often."

The crowd was quiet now, and could not believe what one of their ministers was saying. Then Simmons, the blacksmith arose. "What I have to say may surprise some of you, and may hurt your feelings, but I'm not going to pull any punches," he said. "The Beans are strangers in Palmyra, and there should be a sign over every church door, 'Welcome to the Stranger.'

"Much to the contrary has happened. They have been practically kicked out of two of our churches and have been given to understand that they are not wanted."

Simmons took a deep breath, then added, "I want you to know that the Beans did not impose themselves on us last Saturday, but were there by invitation, by solicitation of myself. They were there as my guests and I promised them and guaranteed to them that they would have our respect. I have done considerable business with Mr. Bean and have conversed with him on many occasions on varied subjects, and as far as general Christian qualities are concerned, he is far above some who have viciously and maliciously falsified him here tonight, as heaven is above hell. I want you to meet and get acquainted with him and know him as I know him. And if he remains in our midst long enough, you will know that what I have said is the truth." [1]

Simmons was certainly not the icon of importance in the community that Mr. Sexton had been, nor did he carry any massive influence. But the words he spoke that evening could not have been orated by anyone any better.

More than ever Willard felt the comforting hand of the Lord over the Church's interest in acquiring the Hill Cumorah. Following Mr. Sexton's funeral, he had thought many times about the sweet counsel he had received from Rebecca reminding him to allow the Lord some time to accomplish His work and purposes. Essentially it was the same counsel he was receiving from Church leaders, and it served as a second witness to validate his present course of non-action.

It had been nearly a month since the passing of Pliny Sexton when Willard received a letter from the Presiding Bishopric of the Church.

One week after the death of Mr. Sexton, his $2,000,000 estate was probated and fell into the hands of his heirs. The Sextons had never had children. In 1881, Mr. Sexton's wife Harriett became the vice-president of First National Bank of Palmyra and the couple devoted their lives to the building of the estate. Following their deaths, with no children to inherit

---

[1] *Willard Washington Bean Autobiography,* 2:26.

CHURCH OF JESUS CHRIST OF LATTER-DAY SAINTS
OFFICE OF THE PRESIDING BISHOPRIC
SALT LAKE CITY, UTAH,

September 23, 1924.

Elder Willard Bean,

Palmyra Farm.

Dear Brother:

Your interesting letter was received and we read it to the Presidency at our meeting yesterday.

We were asked to have you keep us posted in respect to the matter of the Hill Cumorah, and advise us of any developments in connection therewith, but we should not appear too anxious about it. If we use caution and the Lord wants us to have possession of the Hill, it will be so over-ruled. Or, on the other hand, no matter how anxious and how hard we may try, unless the matter is over-ruled in our favor, we will not succeed.

We are always glad to hear from you. Hope you will write often and keep us advised as to the progress of the work under your direction.

Your brethren in the Gospel,

THE PRESIDING BISHOPRIC,

By

CWN/LA.

The Presiding Bishopric's letter to Willard Bean, written on September 25, 1925, urging him to be patient concerning the purchase of the Hill Cumorah.

the holdings, a group of angry heirs banded together to stifle any hope of the Church obtaining the Hill Cumorah. The nearest of kin was a niece who had married a German count by the name of Hans Giese, and an adopted niece, Mrs. Ray. They came together with the other distant heirs with a hate-filled pact, pledging themselves to never sell "Mormon Hill" to the Church for any price.[2]

A year went by, and then another, as Willard began to realize that the Church may never be able to obtain the hill. At every turn Willard found opposition from those who were unfriendly to the Church. With the generosity and friendship of Mr. Sexton gone, the heirs had deliberately placed a staunch anti-Mormon as the tenant of the Sampson farm. This man took great joy at driving away anyone who wanted to visit the hill.

Willard had already received several complaints about the situation, and he was about to receive another as a knock came at the door of the Smith home. Willard rose from his chair and opened it.

"Oh, Elder Bean, I was hoping I would catch you here," the visitor said. "I was a missionary here years ago and brought my family back to sit on top of the Hill Cumorah, but a man with a gun chased us off. I thought those days were gone. We used to hold conferences on the hill, and I thought it would be all right if I just walked up there with my family."

"Please come in, and have your family come in," Willard told him.

"I am sorry, but we are in such a rush that we are out of time and need to be in Syracuse by nightfall," the man said. "I just wanted to make you aware of it. Thank you, and we will try it again in a few years if we get back this way."

[2] Cameron J. Packer, *A Study of the Hill Cumorah*, BYU Master's Thesis, 84–85.

Willard closed the door and went into the kitchen where Rebecca was. "Did you hear that sad tale?" he asked.

"I heard it. It seems to be happening more and more. I wonder if we will be able to keep having our mission conferences there as we have done in the past."

"Oh, we will keep having them, I guarantee you that. Perhaps I ought to put my gloves back on and start swinging. They are throwing punches again and it is hard for me to just sit here and be pummeled without doing anything. I don't think we're just supposed to get backed into a corner and become a punching bag for anyone who wants to swing at us."

Rebecca cautiously smiled her approval and said, "Here's the biggest knife I have in the kitchen, and I'll get your Winchester and wolf poison ready."

Willard shook his head and laughed. That comment was so unlike Rebecca, but he caught her message.

"Don't worry, dear," he assured her. "I'll be civil and kind, if you will be."

Willard left the house, not knowing exactly what he was going to do, but feeling confident he would be guided by the Lord. When he arrived at the Sampson farm, he drew a large breath and headed up the little lane to the home of the lessee, Frank Burgiss. Willard knocked confidently on the door, and immediately found himself face-to-face with the unfriendly tenant.

"Ah, Mr. Bean. What do you want?" the man asked.

"I don't want anything, except for you to listen to me for one minute," Willard said boldly.

"Okay, you've got one minute!"

"I remind you that we own part of the Hill Cumorah, and if you chase any more of our people off that hill, this is what I will do. I will post a big sign on our land down on the state road where your little lane leads up to this house, and on it will say, 'ALL MORMONS—KEEP OFF THE HILL, BY ORDER OF FRANK BURGISS!' Then I will have it photographed by a correspondent of the *Rochester Daily*, who is friendly to us, and it will be published throughout the entire area for all to read. I do not believe that you or your executors will like that kind of publicity, but you do as you like."[3]

The fear of bad publicity silenced the opposition and by the time the executors sent their foreman out to meet with Burgiss, he had already ceased his antagonism. Willard had believed all of his life that the Lord and man, working together, make an unbeatable team.

Early upon Willard's arrival in Palmyra in 1915, he had made acquaintance with an attorney by the name of Charles C. Congdon. They had established a warm friendship over the years and when the Lord was ready, Mr. Congdon was a part of the inner circle of the Sexton heirs as the chief lawyer of the Sexton estate. By December 1927, the timetable of the Lord was on schedule and people were in place to miraculously bring about the purchase of the Hill Cumorah.

It had been four years since the death of Mr. Sexton and in that time some of the more anti-Mormon heirs had also found their way into the spirit world. The remaining heirs were tired of waiting for their inheritance and were anxious to get whatever they could from a sale of the properties. On January 30, 1928, Charles C. Congdon phoned Willard.

"How are you doing this cold, wintry day?" the attorney asked. "Staying warm enough, I hope?"

"Just barely," Willard responded, "like the rest of the state."

"Is there any chance you could come over to my office? I need to talk with you."

---

[3] Cameron J. Packer, *A Study of the Hill Cumorah*, 79.

"I'll come over just as soon as I have finished my lunch," Willard said.

"That's not soon enough," Congdon answered. "I need you to come now, while there is no one in the office, including my secretary."

"Then I'm out the door and on my way," Willard said as he replaced the phone and grabbed for his coat and scarf. He arrived at the lawyer's office on a sprint, and Congdon wasted no time in getting straight to the point.

"Willard, I have just returned from Lyons and have been meeting with the heirs of the Sexton estate, as I do once a year. Mrs. Ray, your chief antagonist, has been very ill, and during the meeting there was no protest registered against the Church buying the Hill Cumorah. We both know that the proper thing would have been for Mr. Sexton to have willed that hill to the Mormon Church, but he didn't. You are the only people who can use that hill, and you ought to have it. Now it's up to us to fix this deal up so they can get what they demand and at the same time arrange so your people can get the worth of your money. The judge tells me if we can complete the deal before any protest is filed, it will be legally binding."

C.C. Congdon

"Let's do it, Charles," Willard said enthusiastically, "and see what happens."

"The heirs are still locked on getting at least $50,000, and I know your Church is willing to pay $35,000. A local man has offered $25,000 and a gentleman from California is offering $30,000, hoping to then sell it to your Church for $35,000. And, as you know, President Fredrick M. Smith of the RLDS Church has been interested in buying the property. So let me tell you my proposal."

Willard exhibited quiet calmness on the outside, but inside his spirit was dancing. He knew what the Lord was doing and could feel the powers of heaven coming together to accomplish what he had been trying to do for over ten years.

"I say we offer the heirs $35,000 for the Sampson Farm," Congdon said. "Then we will offer $10,000 for the Bennett Farm and another $2,000 for the Tripp Farm, bringing our total to $47,000. So we would still be a little short of an acceptable offer to them. Do you have any suggestions?"

Willard mentally walked around the Hill Cumorah in his mind looking for some more available land, but there was none. But another picture flowed quietly into his visual landscape.

"How about the old Grange Hall in town?" Willard asked. "It's a 'white elephant' for them and I know they haven't been able to sell it. We could use it as a chapel, I suppose. Would you say $6000 would be reasonable?"

"Yes it would. Willard, that's a wonderful idea. The Grange Hall never crossed my mind. That makes our offer $53,000, and I think they will accept it! But will your Church leaders agree?"

"I will airmail Church Headquarters today with our proposal. I think they will approve it."

Willard raced out of Mr. Congdon's office and sprinted down Stafford Road. Willard quickly typed a letter to the First Presidency that was soon flying toward Salt Lake City. However, there was no need to hurry. Heaven had already sent the message.[4]

At the very same time that Willard was writing his letter to

4 Cameron J. Packer, *A Study of the Hill Cumorah*, 79.

The old Grange Hall, part of the Pliny Sexton estate.

the First Presidency, they were drafting a telegram instructing him to see the lawyer of the Sexton estate and get a definite offer.

The workings of heaven in this matter were felt strongly by Willard and the leadership of the Church. It was a testimony to them that the time had come for the Church to have possession of the sacred hill.

C.C. Congdon was able to obtain all of the needed signatures of the Sexton heirs, and for the first time in its history the Church owned the hill where ancient and modern prophets had walked, and where the plates of gold had been hidden for centuries.

A letter from the First Presidency to Willard Bean noting the coincidence of their written letters to each other during the purchase of the Hill Cumorah.

CHAPTER 13

The light of day was just beginning to show as Willard reached the base of Hill Cumorah. He had risen early this particular spring morning and had walked the entire distance from the farm to the hill, just as Joseph Smith had done a hundred years before. Today marked 56 years of mortality for Willard, and he continued to pride himself in keeping his body in mint condition.

"I can still run up this hill," he whispered to himself as he set his legs in motion. He jabbed and punched air all the way to the top. The 100 feet up a steep incline to the summit took his breath away, but it felt wonderful to fill his lungs to capacity. He had fought long and hard over the years to help bring Cumorah into the hands of the Church, and no one could chase them off the hill anymore.

Turning slowly, he stood with his hands on his hips, looking out over the vast landscape of the Fingerlakes region of Western New York. He was higher than anything he could see, for there was no hill in view higher than Cumorah. Breathing more steadily now, Willard sat on the very brow of the northernmost part of the hill and waited for the sun to chase away the shadows.

Willard's mind filled with the sacred events that made up the history of the hill. He felt as though he was sitting near the very spot where Moroni himself had stood. He felt his presence, as if he was not alone on the hill at this early hour.

Willard looked over his left shoulder toward the few trees where he and Abraham Silverstein had enjoyed their brief discussion of the box that contained the gold plates and the Urim and Thummim, and where Moroni had met Joseph on four different occasions.

"Where have all of your trees gone, Cumorah?" Willard thought to himself. "Who has stripped you of your beauty, your God-given cloak of mortal splendor?"

Willard could almost see the Prophet Joseph making his way up through the trees of Cumorah in search of a large stone, thick and rounding in the middle, that Moroni had shown him in vision the night before. Willard sat immersed in a vision of his own, and felt the promptings of heaven on the course of action he should take.

Earlier in February, when the Church had purchased the remainder of the hill, he had written the Church authorities about the possibility of reforesting the hill to resemble what it was like in Joseph Smith's day. Approval was given, and for

The east side of the Hill Cumorah in the 1920s, with the northern end of the hill to the right. Visitors can be seen standing on top of the hill.

months now he had been researching the best means to go about replanting the hill with trees. A recent letter from the State Conservation Department at Albany, informed him that the price of evergreen seedlings were $2.00 to $5.00 per thousand.

However, Willard was told his request fell under the "Church Forest Class" and he could have all of the trees he wanted for free, as long as he would be willing to pay for the shipping. He would begin planting in late summer.[1]

Willard was deep in thought as the sun began to stretch hesitantly over the distant hills and trees to the east. A warm projectile of light quickly intensified as the sun continued to rise. He closed his eyes for a moment to feel the radiance of heaven engulf his soul.

"This is a special place," thought Willard to himself. "The entire world needs to know what happened here, and they must want to come. But even if they do come, how will they know it? It is up to us to make it known, to mark it, to identify it. The trees will help, but there is more we can do."

Ideas and inspiration were flowing into Willard's mind. "The hill must be identified," he said to himself, "so that every passerby will hear the hill speak its message."

Willard looked back along the ridge of Cumorah's west side and pictured huge letters spelling out the name CUMORAH. The 42' x 24' letters would be seen from miles around until the trees they were planting crowded them out.

"And when the letters are overrun by trees," Willard said with a smile, "we will have an electric sign spelling out CUMORAH running along the crest of the hill." [2]

Meanwhile, Willard wasn't going to wait until the trees and

[1] *Willard Washington Bean Autobiography*, 2:36.
[2] Packer, "A Study of the Hill Cumorah," 93.

The hedge, planted by Willard, spelling out the word "Cumorah."

hedges arrived to spread the message of the hill's importance. He placed signs, at different times and of varying sizes, along the road near Cumorah for all to see.

Willard arranged for missionaries to help plant the trees, and he worked steadily to be ready for when the help arrived. He had marked hundred of spots where the trees were to be planted, placing a wooden stake where a hole should be dug. A missionary would use the stake to dig the hole and later plant the seedling.

One bright morning the missionaries assembled at the base of the hill, and Willard stood above them, halfway up the slope.

"All right, missionaries, listen up," Willard called out. "Today we are sowers, not reapers. We are well acquainted with the scripture that says, 'as ye sow, so shall ye reap.' You will see no baptisms today from the sowing you will do. And, you probably won't see any in a month or maybe even a year. Then again, maybe you won't ever see a baptism from the sowing you will do today. But, some day, someone will reap a harvest from the seeds you plant today. Not just someone, but many. You write it down and remember it, for it will surely come to pass."

*One of the many signs Willard placed along Highway 21
(Canandaigua Road) identifying the Hill Cumorah, 1930.*

Willard had felt for many years that the hill would be a marvelous missionary tool in sharing the restored gospel. He had voiced his feelings a number of times and even written a letter to Salt Lake City indicating that the hill could do more real missionary work than a dozen field missionaries.[3] Now it was actually beginning to happen.

"Because of your planting today, many will hear and come to an understanding of the gospel and desire to be baptized," Willard said. "Now go forth and dig those holes, plant those little seedlings, and let them grow and fulfill what the prophet Alma talks about in his 32nd chapter."

Over the course of the project, the State Conservation Department would send Willard more than 65,000 little evergreen trees, which he would supplement with 3,000 hardwood saplings dug up from the Sacred Grove. During the next few years local missionaries would plant about 10,000 trees a year.

But the completion of the project was a long way off when Willard returned to the farm close to dusk after that first long

---

[3] Letter, Willard W. Bean to the Presiding Bishopric, 22 April 1929.

day of planting. He made his usual entrance through the back door into the kitchen.

"Evening, my love," Willard said to Rebecca as he reached for his tin cup that was always in the same place. He pushed three or four times quickly on the pump handle, which brought a stream of the coldest water in all of Palmyra pouring from the spout.

"This has to be one of the great inventions of all time, the pump," Willard sighed as he brought the cup to his lips and let the water trickle down his parched throat. "Where would we be without it?"

"I surely don't know," said Rebecca, shaking her head. "But if you find any more gold on Cumorah, some indoor plumbing would be nice."

"More gold?" Willard asked with a puzzled look on his face. "What are you talking about?"

"That's what the neighbors are saying," Rebecca said with a grin. "It's all over town. You're not holding out on me, are you Willard? We are equal partners in this, you know."

"I can't believe it," Willard said. "The rumors of gold in Cumorah are still alive and well."

"Well, you can't blame them, I suppose," answered Rebecca. "All people can see are a bunch of missionaries digging on the hill with stakes, leaving holes all over the place. What are they supposed to think?"

Willard laughed. "The irony of it all is that Joseph really did receive gold from that hill," Willard said. "But the gold is worthless, just like Moroni said. It's the book—the message— that contains the real worth.[3] If only the people would believe it, they would be so rich."

Rebecca nodded in agreement as Willard pumped the

---

[3] *Mormon 8:14.*

handle a few more times and filled his cup again. He shook his head and laughed a little as he drank another glass of what he called "living water." He knew he would thirst again, but it was almost worth it, just to taste the water's soothing power.

"I guess I better put a piece in the newspaper tomorrow so the rumors don't get too out of hand," he said. "One thing we don't need is a gold rush to Cumorah. And I better write to Salt Lake before they get wind of it, or else the Church Audit Committee will be on our front porch before nightfall.[4]"

Willard paused before broaching another subject he had been pondering. "Rebecca dear, what would you think about us opening up a gas station over by Cumorah?"

"Oh sure, Willard," laughed Rebecca, "and I could run over in between fixing meals for our visitors and pump a little gas."

Willard's mind was a little over two miles away as Rebecca's comment seemed to fly right past him.

"You are joking, aren't you Willard?" Rebecca said more seriously. "Please tell me you are joking."

"In between pumping gas," Willard said, "you could repair a few tires, maybe some minor repair work, nothing major of course. We could sell some of that lemonade of yours, and some sandwiches and such. But more than anything else, we could have books and pamphlets about the Church and Cumorah and make it a real missionary stop."

"You really are serious," Rebecca moaned.

Willard nodded. "Yes. Well, about everything I said except you working there, my love. Think of it, the Cumorah Hill Filling Station. There are going to be more and more cars coming. A lot more."

Willard and Rebecca smiled at each other as they sought

---

[4] Letter, Willard W. Bean to the Presiding Bishopric, 23 October 1928.

to remain a little lighthearted about their current conversation. They had always sought to laugh and live, rather than cry and die, and that is why they had more happy days than sad days.

NOW OPEN

Cumorah Hill Filling Station

W. W. BEAN, PROP.

HIGH GRADE
WEBACO GASOLINE
AND OILS

WALBURN
ETHYL GASOLINE

All Kinds of Refreshments
BARBECUE
SANDWICHES
OUR SPECIALTY

ICE CREAM
AND CANDIES

Come Out and See Us

Shown above is Willard's gas station and store on Canandaigua Road on the west side of the Hill Cumorah. (Courtesy of Community of Christ Archives, Independence, Missouri)

To the left is a newspaper advertisement about Willard's new station.

CHAPTER 14

The 10,000 evergreen striplings that were planted on the Hill cumorah in the fall of 1928 were under snow by late November, and the Bean family found itself iced in for the duration of winter. Buggies and automobiles were of little use in the deep snow, so the old sleigh with straight runners pulled behind a good horse was still the vehicle of choice.

Willard spent the winter months at the local libraries, reading and learning and writing. He was an avid reader and student, particularly concerning religion. He wrote a series of articles that was printed in the *Palmyra Courier-Journal* on the history of Palmyra and the beginning of the Church.

The King's Daughter's Library was his favorite place of hibernation during the snow days of winter. While perusing the endless rows of books, Willard discovered a very long shelf filled with negative print and publication against the Church.

"Why are there all these anti-Mormon railings against us?" he asked himself. "Yet there isn't one official word positive about the Church, and not even a Book of Mormon. No wonder people have such ridiculous and false ideas about us."

Willard had wondered many times why there was so much evil and error written about the Church. The father of lies had seemed to work overtime against the Church, spreading every falsehood imaginable to confuse any and all seekers of truth. Willard could not recall ever reading any books published by members of the Church trying to destroy another belief or

The Hill Cumorah under snow.

religion, ridiculing their doctrines, or spreading lies about them. He often wondered why the ignorant and the self-vaunting ones railed on the Mormons more than anyone else.

As Willard left the library that day, he stopped at the librarian's desk.

"Hello, Mr. Bean. How was your time in the library today?" the librarian asked.

"Wonderful, as usual," Willard said. "You're always so helpful to me and I am grateful. Perhaps you can tell me why there is a whole shelf filled with negative things about the Mormon Church, but absolutely nothing official from the Church or anything good that has been written about the Church?"

"That is really interesting," the librarian said. "I really couldn't tell you why that is, but I will bring it up with the Board of Directors when they meet on Monday. I will have an answer for you the next time you are here."

"Thank you," Willard said. "I will be most anxious to hear

their response. Please let them know that I will be happy to donate several official books from the Church that will give a true and actual representation of our beginnings and beliefs."

"That sounds wonderful, Mr. Bean. I will let them know."

Willard bundled up warmly before opening the door and walking out into the New York version of Antarctica. Brownie, his favorite sleigh and buggy horse, was tethered to the ground where Willard had anchored him. The remains of a quarter-bale were still evident on the snow where Brownie had tried to lick up every speck of anything that looked like hay. Willard placed his bag of papers and books in the sleigh next to the remainder of the bale of hay.

"Ho, Brownie, let's go," Willard shouted as the whip popped sharply above the horse's head. "Home, Brownie, home."

Brownie knew the way home and needed no guidance to find his way there. The horse's gentle jog with the mesmerizing mix of the harness bells usually made it easy for Willard to sleep until Brownie stopped in front of the barn door. But this time he couldn't sleep. For some reason, as of late, his mind was continually meandering up and down the slopes of Cumorah. Like a huge magnet, it attracted him, even in the dead of winter. Moroni was very real to him, and the fact that he was living near the very hill this ancient prophet had traversed many times thrilled his soul.

Willard had read everything Moroni had written many times, besides everything that had ever been written by anyone about him. He tried to visualize in his mind Moroni's father, the great prophet Mormon, raising his infant son to the heavens during a priesthood ordinance and pronouncing a name and a blessing. Willard was sure that the name Mormon chose had come directly from the Nephite records describing the incomparable commander of the Nephite armies, Captain Moroni. He was convinced that as Mormon had abridged the

Nephite records, he had written, "If all men had been, and were, and ever would be, like unto Moroni, behold, the very powers of hell would have been shaken forever; yea, the devil would never have power over the hearts of the children of men."[1] Mormon had named his son Moroni, likely hoping he would be an example of righteousness like his ancient predecessor, and Moroni was.

There was still a good deal of daylight left as Old Brownie trotted into the Smith farm and headed for the barn. Willard reined him to the left, however, toward the front of the Smith home.

"Whoa, whoa Brownie," Willard shouted as he pulled hard on the reins, bringing the sleigh to an immediate stop. Jumping quickly to the ground, with the tether in his hand, Willard grabbed Brownie's mane and rubbed his neck hard. "We're not quite through just yet, old friend. Hang on a minute."

Willard rushed to the front door of the home and opened the door with authority. "Children, put on your leggings, bundle up, grab your mittens, and I'll grab your sleds. We're heading to Cumorah. It beckons us, so hurry."

Little screams and laughter filled the inside of the Smith home as the children readied themselves for winter fun. With the sleigh packed high with sleds and children, the harness bells of Old Brownie headed southward on Stafford Road, then easterly to Canandaigua Road, and south again to Hill Cumorah.

The two-mile journey seemed short as Willard caught a view of Cumorah's white summit.[2] "If ever there was a sleigh-riding hill made to perfection," Willard thought, "it had to be Cumorah."

---

[1] Alma 48:17.
[2] Palmyra Bean Packer Interview, January 17, 2007.

For the adventurous sledder, there was the northern slope. It was the steepest and longest. As the hill extended southward the incline softened and the slope became less intense. Anyone, regardless of age, could find a slope to their liking.

Willard knew the sled-riding days on Cumorah were numbered. In just a few short years the trees now beginning to grow would put a sudden end to any such activity. There were other hills where sleds would slide, since the Lord had different activities in mind for this hill.

Before the Church acquired all of the Hill Cumorah in 1928, there had been talk about the possibility of a monument on the crest of the hill. But there was skepticism voiced by some leaders that the continued animosity against the Church would mean that vandalism would be a constant concern.

Discussion of a monument hadn't been mentioned for quite some time, so Willard sought to resurrect the idea. In April 1929, he sat at his desk and wrote a letter to the Presiding Bishopric.

In the letter he wrote, "Now if we had a bureau of information, a MONUMENT on top, part of the ground parked and set out to ornamental shrubs, flowers, lawn, etc. we could begin to divert tourist travel this way, and do more real missionary work than a dozen field missionaries."[3]

While Willard was thinking and writing about a monument on Cumorah, the board of directors of the King's Daughter's Library also knew the power of the pen. In their meeting, Willard's request to have additional books in the library was on the agenda. The head of the board was an old maid whose father had been a revered pioneer minister in the Palmyra area. For more than forty years she had taught school and claimed an avid interest in the welfare of its children.

---

[3] Letter, Willard Bean to the Presiding Bishopric, 22 April 1929.

"The last item on the agenda is Mr. Bean," she said. "As we all know, he's the Mormon who has lived out at the Smith place for quite some time. He wants to know why all the books on our shelves are anti-Mormon and why we don't even have a Book of Mormon or any other book from his Church on our shelves. He wants to give us some as a gift.

"I will just say that as the head of this board I adamantly refuse to even consider having any reading material from the Mormon Church on our shelves. We all know that the object of Mormons everywhere is to sow their diabolical religion among the young people, and we shall not allow it to happen in this library, so long as I have anything to do with it. We shall not discuss it further. Now I move that we bring this meeting to a close and be on our way."[4]

Later that day, Willard hopped up into his sleigh after leaving the post office and headed Old Brownie in the direction of the King's Daughter's Library. He was anxious to hear the board's decision concerning his request. He opened the door and approached the librarian.

"Mr. Bean, I was wondering when you would return," the librarian said. "I have some information for you and I am afraid it is not good. The board has ruled that they will not change any of the books on the shelves and that they will not allow any books contributed by the Mormon Church to be on the shelves. I'm sorry."

"Why am I not surprised?" Willard responded. "I really expected that to be the answer. We'll give it some time. Things will change. I really appreciate you taking it to the board. I know it wasn't easy."

"Think nothing of it, Mr. Bean. We'll keep trying and someday it will happen. I know it will."

---

[4] *Willard W. Bean Autobiography*, 107.

As Willard's letter arrived at Church headquarters, interest and discussions about a possible monument began to elevate among the leaders, but there were still concerns that someone would desecrate it. Willard researched and drew up plans of a protective fence line at an estimated cost of $4,000, but was able to convince Church leaders that it would be a waste of money, and that the Church was quickly gaining the respect and friendship of its new neighbors.[5] While all of this periphery action was taking place, the powers of heaven had already been at work and far ahead of anyone else.

Torlief S. Knaphus, a young convert from Norway and a brilliant young study in the art of sculpture, had immigrated to Utah following his conversion to the gospel. When he learned that the Church owned the Hill Cumorah, he felt overwhelming impressions to start making sketches of a monument honoring the angel Moroni. He finalized seven different sketches, but was unsure what course of action he should take. He hadn't been asked by anyone to prepare or present these images to any of the Church leaders. Should he be so bold, so pretentious? He did not want to appear manipulative in any way. He only knew the impressions he had felt. He was partial to one of the drawings, feeling that it was truly the best one, but he wanted only to please the Lord. He felt impressed to pray and ask for further help and guidance.

Late in the evening Torlief gathered up his sketches and left his home. Past the temple he walked, northward up the road past the state capitol building, veering westward until he found the path. It was a steep incline to the top of Ensign Peak, but it was where he felt he needed to go. It was a sacred place, for he knew that on this very peak the first temple ordinances had been performed in the Salt Lake Valley. There was no

---

[5] Bean, *Willard Washington Bean Autobiography*, 2:37.

temple when the pioneers had entered the valley, but there was
a mountain peak, which would serve as a temple until a sacred
place was built.

Torlief was out of breath as he reached the summit of
Ensign Peak. Lowering his leather satchel to the ground, he
sat beside it and rested as he looked out over the western salt
desert. The moon's rays were shimmering off the Great Salt
Lake as though a host of a trillion fireflies were landing on its
mirror-like surface. There were lights as far as he could see
southward to the end of the valley. He sensed that he truly was
just an observer here, in the constant and evolving grandeur of
God's eternal purposes. He felt his own simple insignificance
and wondered why he, and not someone else, was sitting on this
paltry peak in the desert. He was ready for the help of heaven.

Torlief opened his worn leather satchel. Gently he retrieved
his offering to the Lord and placed his seven sketches in front
of him on the ground, a small pebble keeping each from taking
flight in the wind. He knelt in solemn prayer.

"Dear Father. As thou seest, I approach Thee in humble
prayer, and not entirely sure that I should even be here. Please
forgive me if I am in error, and if my own personal desires rule
my feelings more than Thine. I seek nothing for myself, but
feel only that I am in Thy service and have done Thy bidding.
I present before Thee seven renditions of the ancient prophet
Moroni, whose statue will soon rise above the crest of the Hill
Cumorah so that all might know of Thy special gift to the world,
the Book of Mormon. If it be Thy will, wilt Thou please show
unto Thy servant Thy preference and Thy choice to represent
this grand and glorious event of the dispensation of the fullness
of times. Wilt thou help me see Thy mind and will if truly I am
here to receive of Thy help. Please, Father, I wait before Thee as
one most unworthy. . ."

Torlief testified that when he opened his eyes he was

immersed in light and that he could see all seven drawings positioned on the ground in front of him. He further testified that he saw a finger point to one of the sketches and at the same time heard a verifying voice from heaven that said, "This is the right one."

"But how should I go about presenting this to Thy servants and leaders?" Torlief prayed. "What will they think and how will they know? What should I say to them?"

"All things are in my care. In the morning you shall present yourself at the Church Office Building. You will find the Brethren waiting for you there."

The following morning Torlief went to the Church Office Building as he had been told to do. The authorities of the Church greeted him warmly, as though they were expecting him, and as if the meeting had been planned ahead of time. On a large table in front of him he placed the pictures, one by one, and watched as the Brethren studied each drawing carefully. Finally, following a short discussion, they pointed to the picture that was his own personal favorite, and the same identified the night before on Ensign Peak, as being the right one.[6]

Torlief was overcome with emotion and gratitude to the Lord as he was commissioned by the Church to create a monument honoring the great and last Nephite prophet. For more than fourteen hundred years Moroni, keeper and protector of the gold record, had watched over its resting place, waiting for the day the Lord would bring it forth.

It would not be long before the hill would bear his image, and that a library in Palmyra would finally make a place on its shelf for the record under his charge.

In 1932, Willard received a letter from the new president

---

[6] Rebecca Bean, *An Account of the Palmyra Missionary experiences of Willard W. Bean and Rebecca P. Bean*, 9.

of the board of directors of the King's Daughters Library. He opened it curiously and read, "Some time ago you asked for the privilege of putting a Book of Mormon and other reading matter in our library. The way has now been cleared by the death of the opposition, and your literature will be gladly received." [7]

The board further declared that the librarian should clear any book that mentioned the word Mormon with Willard before it would be allowed on their shelves. They were anxious that no literature on their shelves be offensive to Mormons.

The winds of Palmyra were warming.

---

7 Vicki Bean Topliff, *The Fighting Parson*, 76.

CHURCH OF JESUS CHRIST OF LATTER DAY SAINTS
OFFICE OF THE FIRST PRESIDENCY
SALT LAKE CITY, UTAH

February 6th, 1932.

Mr. Willard W. Bean,
Smith Farm,
Palmyra, N.Y.

Dear Brother Bean:-

   Your letter of the 2nd just received.

   I note what you say in regard to placing the Book
of Mormon in the Kings Daughters Library. It is very grat-
ifying after so long a time that they have reached the conclusion that it would be proper to have the Book of Mormon
on their shelves.

   I have submitted your letter to Brother Talmage
with the request that he forward to you the regular library
copy of the Book for this purpose.

   The historical matter to which you refer has also
arrived. I shall read it with interest and am certain that
it will be of value to us.

   With very best wishes,

    Your brother,

In behalf of First Presidency.

*A letter from the First Presidency to Willard Bean concerning placing a
Book of Mormon in the King's Daughter's Library in Palmyra, New York.*

CHAPTER 15

There was much to do on the farm and around Cumorah to keep Willard busy for the next three years before Torlief Knaphus' monument was erected. It was during this time that Willard thought seriously about increasing the diversity of the farm and thought it would be advisable to fill more of the pastures on the farm with horses. He had been a cowboy part of his life and had never relinquished his feelings of a good saddle to straddle on top of a faithful steed.

"Pliny, I'll need you and Dawn to have our three horses ready in the morning by the time your chores are done. We need to be at the rail station by ten o'clock to get our herd of mustangs."

"Sure thing, Dad," answered Pliny. "I've been waiting for this for a long time."

Several weeks before, Willard had purchased twenty-four horses from a farm in Nevada, and they had been shipped all the way to Palmyra by railcar, arriving late in the evening. Willard wasn't quite sure what to expect but he knew by experience to always expect surprises when working with the animal kingdom.

When he and his two young sons, Pliny and Dawn, arrived at the rail station the next morning he knew he had a problem on his hands. Willard and the boys watched excitedly as the stockyard workers opened the doors of the livestock cars and turned the horses loose into the adjacent corral.

"What do you think, son?" Willard asked as he nudged Pliny.

"They look pretty cantankerous to me, Dad."

"Well, they've been cooped up in those cars for days with little water and food and no chance to move around. And they still probably have a lot of wild oats left in them from their days in Nevada. They are a frisky bunch, indeed. We'll let them kick around here in the corral for a while and fill their bellies with water and then we'll get the job done."

The rail station manager walked up alongside Pliny and Dawn then looked over at their dad as the horses bucked and snorted and kicked in the dust.

"Willard, just how are you fixin' to get all these horses from here out to your farm? It looks downright impossible to me and I reckon that at least half of them will be scattered throughout Pennsylvania before nightfall."

"Henry, that sounds like pure Eastern logic to me," Willard said. "I'll tell you exactly how we're going to do it. On the open range, when we move a herd of horses we drive them. We let them know who is boss. If there is an ounce of fear in you, a horse can spot it mile away, same as an opponent in the ring. So, you never show your fear. Or better still, just don't have any fear."

Willard added, "I know you don't want a sermon because you've heard some of mine before, but I'm going to give you one anyway. Joseph Smith, who lived in your city, said that 'Fear and faith cannot exist in the same person at the same time.' So I'm going to use faith, which Joseph Smith says is a principle of action, and drive those horses to the farm, fearlessly. And you know, Henry, I am not afraid of those horses."

"Willard, I do think that is the best sermon you have ever given, probably because it was so short. If you've got a collection cup handy, I'll drop in a half-dollar."

"Thanks, Henry, but you know we have no paid ministry in the Church. It's all free."

"Willard, you are something else! Maybe that's why I like you now, even though I used to hate you. You are always so darn practical."

Willard slapped Henry on the back. "I take that as a kind compliment. Let me show you how my boys and I are going to drive this herd. See that chestnut stallion over there that seems to be bossing all the others around? I've been watching the herd for awhile. He's their leader. They respect him and they follow him. I am going to rope him and have him run right along close to me. The rest of the herd will follow, and those few who stray a little along the way, my boys will chase them back into the pack. That's how we do it."

"All right, we'll get out of your way," Henry said. "When you're ready, they're all yours."

Willard finished explaining the plan to his sons as he mounted his horse and broadened the loop on his lariat. It was easy lassoing the lead horse because there was nowhere to run in a small corral. But once they were out of the corral, they were off to the races. They roared down Main Street on a prayer and a cloud of dust. For many in Palmyra it was the first real horse stampede that they had ever seen, and Willard thought it would be an exciting opportunity for them to have the experience. He made no apologies. He just did it. There was nothing wrong with the East meeting the West, and he knew that both could learn from each other.[1]

Making the turn south on Stafford Road was a bit tricky but Pliny and Dawn finally gathered them all in and the stampede rumbled again as they raced southward out of the city toward an awaiting pasture.

---

[1] Vicki Bean Topliff, *The Life Story of Alvin Pliny Bean*, 10.

"Close that gate, Pliny, and lock it good," Willard shouted. "We'll let them get used to their new home for a while before we put iron to them. Well done, boys, well done!"

While Willard was farming and ranching and preaching for the next two summers, Torlief Knaphus was working on the statue and monument. It was a time-consuming task. It was not easy finding someone to pose as a model that represented, in Torlief's mind, the rugged yet prophetic look of the angel Moroni.

After much deliberation, Torlief prayerfully decided that James Henry Moyle, president of the Eastern States Mission, looked more like Moroni than anyone else. Other models were used for different portions of the statue, but the likeness of President Moyle and the finished monument is remarkable.[2]

There was much to do to prepare the hill for the arrival of the monument. Willard knew that sometimes plans that are made on the top floors of office buildings do not include how it is all going to happen.

Photographs of James Henry Moyle and the Angel Moroni Statue.

---

[2] Cameron J. Packer, *A Study of the Hill Cumorah*, 107.

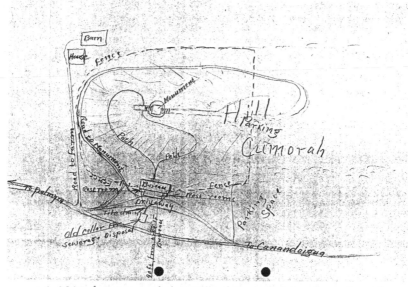

*A 1939 drawing made by Willard Bean showing the paths and
roads on the Hill Cumorah. (Courtesy of LDS Church Archives)*

"How are we going to get the monument up there?" Willard
asked himself. "I know we believe in miracles, but I don't think
we can ask the Lord for another one. We've got to take it from
here."

Willard had already made two paths to Cumorah's summit
to allow visitors a more ready access to the general location
where Joseph Smith had received the plates. These paths had
been paved in places with flagstone, and they converged almost
exactly where the monument was to be placed. However, they
were not wide enough and were too steep for heavy machinery
or trailers to transport such a large monument. Willard walked
all around the hill, thinking, visually surveying the slope, the
terrain, and the projected landscape and future aesthetics of the
entire hill.

Willard had a surveyor friend help him stake out the hill
at a 6 percent grade, starting on the west side of the northern

base. It gradually looped around the north rim, elevating slowly all along the east side, curled around the lower south end, and then headed north along the crest of the hill on a straight shot to where the monument would be placed.

With an iron beamed plow and scrapers drawn by his farm horses, Willard, his sons, and few friends carved a road around Cumorah to the summit on the northern end. It took weeks of sweat and muscle to accomplish the task. Consequently, many of them thought that Moroni's first visit to Joseph Smith on the hill in 1823 had to be a whole lot easier than the one they were planning for now.[3]

As the time drew nearer for the monument's arrival, a decision was made to provide a lighting system that would illuminate the statue atop Cumorah into the far reaches of the night. The only problem was that there weren't any power lines extending from Palmyra as far south as Cumorah.

"Merely an inconvenience," Willard would say. "Problems stop things, but an inconvenience just slows things down a little. All we have to do is have the line extended. That's simple enough."

Permission was slow in coming and time was running out before the dedicatory services that were scheduled for July 21-23, 1935. Willard's constant efforts met deaf ears as he tried to persuade Rochester Gas and Electricity of the necessity of having power for the July services.

Willard knew all too well the age-old adage that "It's not what you know, but who you know." Thankfully, years earlier he had established a close friendship with a Mr. Soderholm, a very influential man in the community. Willard asked if he would accompany him to the Rochester Gas and Electricity Company and help plead the Church's case. He did, and electricity flowed

---
[3] *Willard Washington Bean Autobiography*, 2.

The Angel Moroni statue arrives at the Hill Cumorah.

to Cumorah for the first time in the history of the world.[4]

Foundations were laid, cement was poured, and the trucks had delivered all of the parts of the monument. Torlief Knaphus had arrived to personally supervise the placement and construction of the monument and spent the ensuing evenings at the Smith home with the Beans.

During this time he shared with them his experience of the visitation on Ensign Peak and his meeting with the Church leaders the following morning. Rebecca was truly touched by Torlief's account of the coming forth of the Angel Moroni statue. She asked him, "Was it Moroni who pointed out the picture to you on Ensign Peak that night?"

Torlief smiled gently as he looked back into her eyes. "That's my secret," he said, as though he had shared too much already.[5]

---

[4] Letter, Willard Bean to the Presiding Bishopric, 18 June 1935.
[5] Rebecca Bean, *An Account of the Palmyra Missionary Experiences of Willard W. Bean and Rebecca P. Bean,* 9.

*Torlief Knaphus, left, with Willard and Rebecca Bean as they look
at the Angel Moroni statue on the summit of the Hill Cumorah.*

When it was discovered that the Vermont granite base of
the monument weighed more than 50 tons, Willard was forced
into widening the previous road he had made and hard finish
the surface with rock and gravel.

On May 27, 1935, the 10' 4" statue of Moroni was lowered
into place and anchored securely. But there was concern that
the design for connecting the statue to the base did not take
into consideration the powerful winds gusting up the west side
of the hill. The statue would likely not withstand the shifting
stress of the wind.

The problem was solved by drilling a hole in the armpit of
the statue. Through that hole and another hole already in place
for the lightning-rod cable, they poured liquid cement to give
the statue enough weight to offset the wind.

Now that the statue was finally in place, Moroni stood
majestically, his right hand pointing upward to heaven, his left
hand clutching the gold record which he brought forth.

The day before the statue was anchored, Willard, without any fanfare or ceremony, placed inside the granite monument a time capsule he had made. It included a copy of the Book of Mormon with Moroni's farewell address underlined. He also included a copy of a speech delivered by a Cayuga chief before the New York Historical Society in 1830, and a collection of doctrines taught by a Seneca chief born about 1735.

The Seneca chief recorded that he was taught by three heavenly messengers who said he would be visited by a fourth messenger at a later time. These messengers taught him that in the beginning there were two brothers, one good and one evil. They also taught him of the immortality of the soul, and the everlasting nature of the family united together and living in a sphere of everlasting foliage with fruit of every variety.

Willard also added to the capsule some photographs of the Hill Cumorah, the Sacred Grove, and Joseph Smith's bedroom. At last, the monument was ready to be dedicated.

On the side of the Hill Cumorah a temporary stage and platform area was constructed, covered by a large tent where

One of the dedicatory services of the Angel Moroni Monument, which were held July 21-23, 1935.

Four missionary trumpeters at the Moroni Monument dedication.

speakers and dignitaries would sit during the dedication. Rows of seating stretched in a northwesterly direction to accommodate the many members, missionaries, and guests.

A myriad of photographers and newspaper reporters came from local and national affiliates to be a part of the events. The citizens of western New York were about to experience the largest gathering of Mormons they had ever seen.

Rebecca asked her husband, "Where on earth are we going to put everyone? We have over 400 missionaries and guests coming plus hundreds of others. They'll be sleeping in the fields and in the trees. What are we going to do?"

Willard assured her, "As President of the Lion's Club I have requested their help on this issue. They have responded very favorably. Tomorrow I meet with my fellow members of the Chamber of Commerce and I am sure they will honor our request. I have put the word out through the Agricultural Committee for help with boarding rooms for our visitors, and even some of the ministers are asking their congregations to assist us. This is a miracle, my dear, truly a miracle. They will all have places to stay."

There was a beautiful sunrise on the morning of July 21, 1935, followed by the first dedicatory service at 10 a.m. That service began with a bugle call sounding forth from the summit of Cumorah, followed by four missionary trumpeters playing "The Nephite Lamentation."

Following speeches by the mission president, Don B. Colton, Rudger Clawson of the Council of the Twelve, and David O. McKay of the First Presidency, President Heber J. Grant arose. He made a few remarks, and offered the dedicatory prayer.

President Heber J. Grant offering the dedicatory prayer.

As part of the prayer he said, "We are thankful above all things for the restoration to the earth, of the priesthood, the power to minister in the name of Thine only Begotten Son, which has been given to us of Thee, and by the authority of that priesthood, O, Father, and in the name of our Redeemer, we dedicate unto Thee at this time this monument that has been erected upon this sacred hill.

"We dedicate the hill itself and the ground surrounding it and all of the materials that have been used in this monument; and we humbly pray unto Thee that it may be preserved from the elements, and that it may stand here as a testimony of God, of Jesus Christ, and of the dealings of Jesus Christ with the people that lived anciently upon this continent." [6]

Willard had suggested to the Church authorities that it would be a nice gesture to invite a prominent citizen or two from the community to give some remarks. Though there was some hesitancy on the part of some Church leaders, he assured them that feelings had changed in Palmyra, and that public sentiment had become more than friendly. He was convinced that it would a blessing to everyone, and he received permission to make the invitations. [7]

"This is the office of Judge S.N. Sawyer of Wayne County," answered the receptionist. "How may I help you?"

"Yes, this is Willard Bean calling and I would very much like to speak with Judge Sawyer if he is available."

"Hello, Mr. Bean," responded the secretary. "It is good to hear your voice again. Judge Sawyer will be happy to talk with you, but I must ask you to keep your conversation brief. He has been quite ill lately and his activity is somewhat limited. I will patch you through to him."

"Hello, Willard, you good man, how are you doing?" Judge Sawyer said.

"Just fine, really fine."

[6] Cameron J. Packer, *A Study of the Hill Cumorah*, 119.
[7] *Willard Washington Bean Autobiography*, 2:37.

"Looks like some big doings for your people are coming up here real soon," the judge said. "I've been reading about the big celebration planned for the monument on the hill. How wonderful to see it all come to this."

"It is wonderful, Judge, and that is partly why I am calling. You have been a kind friend to me and our people for many years, and on behalf of the Church I would like to invite you to represent the community and say a few words at our dedication of the monument on Sunday, the 21st of July. We would love to have you a part of it."

"Willard, I esteem it a great honor to represent the people of New York and be a part of your celebration. That is, if I can get my doctor to consent. I'll work on that, though, so don't you worry. If for some reason I can't, I'll dictate something to my secretary and she can read it that day. How's that?"

Willard finished his conversation with the judge and smiled as he realized how many wonderful people he had become friends with since coming to Palmyra. Judge Sawyer was one of the most influential people in all of western New York, as was Judge Thompson, who would also be asked to speak. The dedicatory celebration would soon begin, and Willard could hardly wait.

Willard was so happy to see Judge Sawyer, feeble as he was, attend the dedication. In early June, the judge had written Willard a letter indicating he would not be able to be in attendance due to bad health. But here he was. Willard reached down to take the judge's arm and assist him to the stand as his daughter assisted on the other arm.

"Judge Sawyer, I am so pleased that you are here today," Willard said as he pulled him close for a gentle embrace. "It would not have been the same without you."

"I am pleased to be here too, Willard, and God willing, you'll get a word or two out of me besides."

"Come, dear friend," Willard told him, "let me introduce you to some of our Church leaders."

Willard approached the prophet. "President Grant, I would like you to meet one of my dear friends, Judge Nelson Sawyer from Wayne County, who just happens to be one of the best friends the Church has in this part of the country."

President Grant and Judge Sawyer locked arms as though they had been friends forever and looked into each other's eyes. "Judge Sawyer, words cannot express our deep gratitude to you for your courageous help and kindness to us over the years. I personally, and also on behalf of the Church, extend to you our heartfelt appreciation, not only for being here today on this special occasion, but for all you have done in making this day become a reality. We are indebted to you forever. Please shake hands with my counselor, David O. McKay, and with Rudger Clawson, of the Quorum of the Twelve."

When called upon to speak, Judge Sawyer gave an inspired address concerning the Church and how he had changed his mind about the Mormon people since the Bean family had come to Palmyra. His remarks were so impressive and favorable that the Church printed his entire speech in the *Deseret News* a few weeks later.[8]

As the sun surrendered its light and warmth on the last day of the dedicatory services, electricity kept Cumorah aglow for the first time. From as far as the eye could see, Moroni stood atop a white granite shaft of light shooting upward into the night, and signifying to all that the great God of heaven and earth still speaks to His children.

*

---

8 *Journal History*, 10 August 1935.

A 1935 photograph of the monument at night.

The monument's granite base is surrounded by scaffolding in preparation for the placement of the Moroni statue.

The Moroni statue is carefully hoisted to the top of the granite base.

The Moroni statue is placed on top of the granite base.

Below, a quartet of missionary trumpeters are practicing for their performance during the monument dedication.

*Above, President
Don B. Colton
copies Moroni's
pose as missionaries
stand in front of
the monument.*

*Missionaries and
guests mingle after
the dedication.*

Above, missionaries and guests stand near the base of the monument following the dedication. Palmyra Bean is in the center of the photo wearing a white hat.

A group of missionaries at the base of the monument, including Thane J. Packer (top row, second from right). Elder Packer was one of the trumpeters at the dedication and would later marry Palmyra Bean.

CHAPTER 16

The true beginnings of the Hill Cumorah Pageant started to emerge in July 1926 when a skit was performed on the Joseph Smith farm. Norma Fairbanks, a sister missionary, wrote a short play that was presented on the slopes of the hill behind the Smith home. Young Pliny, only eight years old, was asked to take the part of fourteen-year-old Joseph Smith at the time of the First Vision.

"Mother, I just don't want to play the part of Joseph Smith," Pliny complained.

"Why don't you want to play the part of the prophet?" Rebecca asked. "It would be such an honor and privilege for anyone to have that part."

"I know, Mother. I just don't want to do it, that's all."

"Well, you just think about it, and pray about it," she encouraged. "Then we'll talk about it some more in a few days."

"All right, but I still don't want to be Joseph Smith."

"Run along now while I finish getting supper ready," she told him. "Elder B.H. Roberts is eating with us tonight, and I know you'll like that."

Of all of the general authorities that visited the Smith home, Pliny enjoyed a special relationship with Elder Roberts. The Church leader took a real interest in the boy, and they were inseparable when together.

As they finished their meal that night, Elder Roberts said, "Sister Bean, the meal was just as it always has been—out of

Elder B.H. Roberts sitting with Pliny Bean.

this world. It's really the main reason I come here so often, you know."

"Thank you very much, Elder Roberts. We're not through quite yet, however. Palmyra, please help me pass out the dessert to everyone."

"Sister Bean, if this is some of your berry pie," Elder Roberts said as he winked at Pliny, "I'll take an extra large piece, if you don't mind."

Excitement reigned as everyone received a generous portion of the world's finest pie, the berries for it having been picked that morning by the children along the old rock fence lines behind the Smith home.

"Pliny, pass me that sugar bowl, will you, son?" Elder Roberts asked quickly.

Pliny, his eyes opening widely, watched with covetous amazement as Elder Roberts put six heaping teaspoons of sugar on his pie. Rebecca knew what was coming.

"Mother, can I have as much sugar on my pie as Elder Roberts does?"

"No, Pliny, you cannot," said Rebecca, catching a chagrined smile from Elder Roberts.

Pliny enjoyed his sugarless pie anyway, but always wondered why his mother did not reprimand Elder Roberts the same way she did him. He would understand someday.[1]

---

1 Vicki Bean Topliff, *The Life Story of Alvin Pliny Bean*, 15.

While hanging around Elder Roberts the next day, Pliny decided to receive some apostolic council to his dilemma.

"I'm not too excited about this play thing, Elder Roberts. They want me to play Joseph Smith and I'm not old enough to play him. Besides, I don't want to anyway."

"Well now, that's an interesting fix you're in, lad. Just why is it you don't want to play the part of one of the greatest boys ever to come to earth? Tell me why."

"Well, I just don't like doing stuff like that, and I get all scared in front of people. Someone else could do a lot better. And I . . .," Pliny hesitated, "I just don't want to talk with no angel. I don't even want to see one."

"Ah, so that's it," chuckled Elder Roberts. "My boy, you're not going to need to worry about that at all. Trust me on this one. You are not going to have to talk with any angel."

"Are you sure? I really don't want to, and that's what Joseph Smith did. Angels came, and he talked with them."

"You are right, Pliny. Angels did come to him, so there's no need for them to come to you. They may dress someone up like an angel, but it won't be a real one."

"Well, okay then. I'll play Joseph Smith just as long as I don't have to see an angel."[2]

Echo Hill was directly behind the Joseph Smith home, and it provided a perfect setting for these early pageants. A small set was constructed near the apple orchard, and the audience found a comfortable spot on the side of the hill to watch.

Every July 24th, missionary conferences were held in the Sacred Grove and at Cumorah and the play would generally take place around lunchtime. A meal would be prepared in the barn and handed to everyone so the visitors could eat and watch at the same time.[3]

[2] Vicki Bean Topliff, *The Life Story of Alvin Pliny Bean*, 120.
[3] Palmyra Bean Packer Interview, 17 January 2007.

An audience sits on Echo Hill to watch a play about the Restoration.
The apple orchard and Smith home are in the foreground, 1930.

While Willard was serving as the president of the Lion's Club, the decision was made to sponsor the local high school band and outfit them all with classy uniforms and instruments. The band held concerts every Saturday night in the park that Mr. Sexton had willed to the city, and Willard thought it would be a good idea to have them play and provide music for the Eastern States Missionary Conference.

Some of the other churches in the area complained, so Willard recommended that during the conference the band put on a concert for everyone in the city. The Church would provide other musical numbers interspersed between the band numbers, since there was an abundance of musical talent among the missionaries.

Willard followed up on the idea with James Henry Moyle, the Eastern States Mission President. He reported, "Things are moving ahead nicely with the band concert in the city that we talked about previously. It should be a wonderful missionary opportunity for us when you are here for the mission conference next month."

"Elder Bean, I wish I felt as good about it as you do," President Moyle replied. "I fear that nobody is going to come and that it will be a great embarrassment to the Church. I'm thinking we ought to cancel it and just stay to ourselves out at the farm, like we have done in the past."

Willard was undeterred. "President, trust me. This is going to be an outstanding event. It will be good for us to mix and get acquainted with the people of Palmyra and the surrounding area. The city of Palmyra is willing, and we should be, too. They are becoming friendlier than we are, and by golly, we ought to be as at least as friendly as they are, and more. You won't have to do a thing, except be there. The Lion's Club will do all of the advertising and getting things ready. I guarantee we'll have 1,000 people there."

President Moyle raised his eyebrows. "Wow, 1,000 people? That would be really something if that many people showed up. I just have a hard time believing that."

"I wouldn't be surprised to see 2,000 people there."

"Now you are really off on a tangent, Elder Bean," President Moyle exclaimed, throwing his hands up in the air. "I'll believe it when I see it!"

The night arrived and hundreds of cars and citizens filled the streets and sidewalks. The people flocked to the park to enjoy an overflow concert. Missionaries talked with villagers, and villagers shook hands with missionaries as music entered their ears. Everyone was in good spirits.

President Moyle almost shouted for joy when he learned that over 3,000 people attended the concert that evening.[4]

---

4 *Willard Washington Bean Autobiography*, 2:34.

An early pageant set at the base of the Hill Cumorah.

From these humble beginnings the Hill Cumorah began to make itself ready for a much more impressive and extravagant production. In 1936, an audience of five thousand people sat on the side of Hill Cumorah and watched as 70 missionaries acted out a production entitled *Truth From The Earth*.

The following year, a young missionary assigned to the Eastern States Mission became involved in the production as an assignment from his mission president. Thus began a long legacy of service in which Harold I. Hansen would develop the pageant to much of its present grandeur.

Cast members prepare for one of the early pageants on Cumorah.

CHAPTER 17

The winter of 1938 was fairly typical for western New York, but Rebecca's health had kept her down a little and Willard's somersaults were nowhere to be seen. He had celebrated his 70th birthday during the previous spring. The Beans were into the 25th year of their five-year calling, and were looking forward to spending the remainder of their lives among the people they had loved for so many years.

In February 1939, Willard sat down at his desk and thumbed through a stack of mail that had been delivered to their home. As always, he looked first for any letters from Salt Lake City, giving them his immediate attention.

Willard noticed a familiar envelope and quickly eyed the left corner of the envelope, which showed the mark of the Office of the First Presidency. Willard reached calmly for his letter opener and sliced a clean cut along the top edge of the envelope. Unfolding the typewritten letter inside, he began to read. The message wasn't a knockout punch, for he had never been knocked out, but it was a blow that staggered him just a little.

Willard read the release letter from the First Presidency and wept. He had never done a lot of crying in his life and didn't possess a whole lot of patience with men who did. But sometimes there are things that ought to moisten one's eyes.

"Where has it all gone?" Willard thought to himself as he continued to blink away the tears. "It was but a week ago when

CHURCH OF JESUS CHRIST OF LATTER DAY SAINTS
OFFICE OF THE FIRST PRESIDENCY
SALT LAKE CITY, UTAH

HEBER J. GRANT, PRESIDENT
J. REUBEN CLARK, JR., FIRST COUNSELOR
DAVID O. McKAY, SECOND COUNSELOR

February 2, 1939

Elder Willard W. Bean
Palmyra, New York

Dear Brother Bean:

For twenty-five years you and Sister Bean have labored well and faithfully as missionaries at Palmyra, New York. When you first accepted this responsibility misunderstanding of the Church and prejudice generally against the Mormon people were rampant. Constantly to meet such antagonism was not a pleasant nor an easy task. Less determined and less capable missionaries would have become discouraged, if not disheartened.

However, by patience, kindness, and discretion, and divine guidance to which you were entitled, you won your way into the hearts of the people with whom you associated. During your administration of Church affairs at Palmyra and vicinity you have seen enmity and suspicion replaced by the spirit of tolerance and friendliness and historic spots become shrines marked by appropriate and enduring monuments. Your opportunities to proclaim the restored Gospel have been many, and the satisfaction and joy that accompany such labors you have experienced in high degree.

Yours has been a special duty, consequently you have been kept longer at your post of service than have others regularly called into the mission field.

At last, however, with appreciation of your loyalty and faithfulness and with commendation for your accomplishments during these years of devotion, we now extend to you and Sister Bean an honorable release from your assignment at the Sacred Grove and the Joseph Smith Farm.

The time of your returning to Utah will be left to your convenience. Unless you have some other vocation in mind we shall be pleased to have you spend part of your time at the Bureau of Information in Salt Lake City. For this part-time service you will be given an allowance of $100.00 per month.

Elder and Sister Merle Ellis have been appointed to succeed you on the Farm. Undoubtedly later a missionary will be chosen to meet the people who visit the Sacred Grove, and to take care of the house, which should be preserved for its historic and sacred interest.

Again expressing appreciation of your faithfulness to the important assignment that has been yours, and ever praying for your continued success and happiness, we remain,

Sincerely yours,
THE FIRST PRESIDENCY

By _J. Reuben Clark Jr._
David O. McKay

Willard and Rebecca Bean's release letter from the First Presidency.

we arrived, and now they say it is time to go home. What has happened to our life? Where has it vanished to?"

Willard's mind rehearsed the memorable words of Jacob in the Book of Mormon as he tried to put a clock on the last third of his life, "the time passed away with us, and also our lives passed away like as it were unto us a dream." [1]

---

1 *Jacob 7:26.*.

It had truly been a dream, a good dream, the kind of dream one hopes will never end. But mortality is structured on a framework of endings, and Willard had always understood that a round always ends at the sound of the bell, regardless of one's desire to fight on.

Willard clasped the letter in his hand as he rose slowly from his chair and walked into the kitchen where Rebecca had spent most of the last 288 months of her life. He handed her the letter as he sat down at the kitchen table and watched. There was suspicion in her eyes.

It only took a moment before more tears began flowing. Rebecca brought her hand quickly to her mouth as she sat down in a chair next to Willard and continued to read. Soon her tears were mixed with gentle sobs until finally she was unable to see another word.

Willard stood and pulled his beloved companion up into his arms and held her close for as long as was needed. This was not something they had anticipated. They had convinced themselves in recent years that their final resting place would be in the Palmyra Cemetery.

"It was just yesterday," whispered Willard, "when I was walking into that stake conference back in Richfield and noticed my bride sitting there in the choir seats. You smiled at me when I saw you. We thought that was going to be just a regular, normal day, didn't we?"

"I will never forget the shock of hearing President Smith call out your name from the pulpit," Rebecca said. "He asked you to come to the stand. Little did we know then what lay ahead, and little do we know now, but there is one thing I do know. We are in His hands, and we came because of Him, and now we leave because of Him."

Through Willard's mind raced a lightning replay of the many

bridges that had been built over the past 24 years between the Church and the community. The Beans were as much a part of Palmyra as any family, and respect for the Church had grown in size from mouse to mammoth.

They talked of the community banquet held last month. "Willard, why are you and Mrs. Bean sitting down here in the audience?" the Reverend had asked. "We have a place for you up at the ministers' table. Here are your tickets and your plates and you are always to be up there with us."

"We are perfectly comfortable being down here," Willard explained, "and to pay for own meal."

The Reverend shook his head. "We are not comfortable with that and we want you up front. I have been assigned by my fellow clergymen to bring you forward and join us." [2]

Willard smiled as he thought of the hand of friendship extended from the clergy of other faiths. Remarkable as it seemed, it was a miracle that was supposed to happen.

It did not take long for the entire community of Palmyra and surrounding area to hear the news. It was a shock and a disappointment and many of them registered their verbal complaints against the Church for taking away two of their most respected citizens. Willard was hoping to leave without any fanfare and slip away quietly into the night, but members and non-members alike would not be robbed of a final farewell to a couple they had truly come to love.

The Palmyra Branch joined with the Rochester and Canandaigua Branches of the Church and gave the Beans a farewell sendoff. The local residents and surrounding communities were not to be outdone by the members of the Church. They were not ready to give them up that quickly.

---

[2] *Willard Washington Bean Autobiography*, 3:28. Willard further records that his minister friends would often stop and visit him in Utah during their travels.

Festivities were planned and the Beans were the major focus. The Lion's Club, of which Willard was a charter member, held a banquet with entertainment and speakers and presented a framed testimonial of gratitude with all of their names attached. As the gift was presented, the president spoke.

"We are doing honor to a family that came to Palmyra some years ago. When they settled on the Joseph Smith farm, some of our super-pious citizens started a tirade with the object of getting rid of them. But as they proved themselves good citizens, we soon learned to tolerate them, then we learned to admire and respect them, and now we love them. It is with reluctance that we now bid farewell to the most versatile family that ever lived in Wayne County." [3]

The Chambers of Commerce of Rochester and Palmyra next joined together and rented the high school auditorium and kitchen for a huge banquet and program honoring the Beans. Many compliments and honors flew their way as they had the previous night, but the most touching farewell of all came on their last night in Palmyra, when those who were not members of any high-class or civic organizations came together.

Villagers from four different counties, rich and poor, the commoners of the community who were just normal, salt-of-the-earth people, met to shake hands one last time with the Beans. Many had heard Willard preach on Saturday evenings over the years, and this night he would deliver his final sermon to them. He would tell them of the afterlife and what lay beyond our mortal lives. Many tears were shed and people lingered way into the night.

About 8:30 p.m. a messenger arrived, handing Willard a small, white envelope. He excused himself briefly from conversation and opened the envelope. The letterhead at the

---

3 Vicki Bean Topliff, *The Fighting Parson*, 84.

top of the note showed the name "Judge S.N. Sawyer" followed by a brief message: "Do not leave Palmyra without calling on me."

The judge's quarters were only a block away, and Willard sent word back with the messenger that he would visit the judge come at 10 p.m. As the evening of honor continued and the hour of his appointment with Judge Sawyer approached, he pulled Rebecca aside.

"Dear, it is imperative that I go and visit Judge Sawyer for a few minutes. Cover for me till I get back and I'll return just as soon as I can." [4]

"I'll do the best I can Willard, but you must get back here as soon as you can. People will wonder where you are."

"I know, I know. I won't be long."

Willard did a 70-year-old jog down the street and was quietly ushered into where his dear friend was sitting comfortably in a large, reclining leather chair. Judge Sawyer had planned a little party of his own and had invited C.C. Congdon, executor of the Sexton estate, and his wife, plus some other family members.

"Thank you for coming," the judge said. "It means so much to me. I so wanted to see you again before you left."

"Thank you, Judge. I am so honored that you asked me to come. I would not have left town without coming to see you."

The judge motioned to the others. "You know the Congdons, I am sure, and the rest of my family welcomes you."

Willard reached out and grabbed the hand of C.C., the major player involved in the Church acquiring the Hill Cumorah. Willard thought how ironic that here he was, in the presence of two noble and honorable men of the law and a credit to their profession, when in Joseph Smith's day there was not an honest lawyer to be found anywhere to help the Church.

---

4 *Willard Washington Bean Autobiography*, 2:37.

The judge continued, "As you know, Willard, my wife Agusta passed away a short time ago, and my loneliness is almost more than I can bear. I miss her terribly and cannot stand the thought of being without her. So, I wanted to see you again before you left for Salt Lake City and were gone forever from my life."

Judge Samuel Nelson Sawyer
(Photo courtesy of the New York State Supreme
Court, Appellate Division, Fourth Department
Law Library, Rochester, New York)

As the judge spoke, Willard was overwhelmed with a feeling that he was in this home this evening not to just say good-bye, but that he was on God's errand and had been sent with a message to give.

"Judge, it is not by accident that we are together this evening," he said. "You were inspired to send a messenger and have me come and I come with a message. Listen to me carefully, for I have something important to share with you. I understand the great feelings of love you have for your wife and dear companion and the feelings of yearning that you have for her. I know your thoughts and I know your worries. I know you have been taught all your life that you were married to her only until you die. Well, it's not true. God has revealed to the earth further light and knowledge on this issue."

Judge Sawyer rose slightly in his chair as if he was hearing for the first time that which he had hoped for and believed for a long time, but had never found.

"It will not be long," Willard continued, "until you are with your sweet wife again. Yes, my dear friend, you will be together again. You will be taught some things when you get there, but you need to know now that you will be as near and dear to each other there as you have been here in your earthly tabernacles. It is the eternal plan, the continuation of family relationships. It is the way of God."

"But why have I not heard this, Willard. Where is this doctrine? Where is it taught?"

"It is why Joseph Smith was needed. There have been many great truths lost from the earth over the ages because of Satan's influence. But God our Father loves us and has restored truths and ordinances back to the earth again so we can know these things. It makes us happy to know these things, and our Heavenly Father wants His children happy."

Judge Sawyer's countenance began to brighten a little as he stared straight into Willard's eyes, almost pleading for more.

"Think with me for a minute," continued Willard. "Why, in all of the eternities, would the great God in heaven, our Father, want to bring an end to a family? Why, in anyone's wildest imagination, would God want to sever and destroy the sacred bond of love established between a husband and a wife?

Satan would, but not the Father. Not a Father who loves His children."

The judge asked, "You're saying I will be with my wife again, that she is waiting for me, and that we will be together forever?"

"Yes, it is true. It is as right as rain, and God is the author of it," Willard said.

"Do you know this for a fact, or is this just something you are saying to make an old man feel better?"

Willard looked the judge in the eye and said, "I know, beyond any earthly thing I know, that this is true. I have never known anything more than I know this. And I will tell you something else I know. You and I, sitting here talking together, are having our last visit in the flesh, and that we have had a happy time together over the years. I will soon follow you and your good wife into the world of spirits where our friendship will be renewed and be just as real as it is here on earth. You have been a great friend to many here on the earth and that will be to your blessing over there. Your associations here will continue there."

The judge noticeably relaxed as he pondered the words that Willard had just shared with him. Throughout his life as a judge, he had learned that after the evidence was presented and weighed, the verdict seemed to speak for itself.

"You need not have any anxiety or fear about dying," comforted Willard. "We all have to do it to get there. I feel to say to you that you will not have any prolonged suffering as your time arrives and that you will pass peacefully and quietly away as if you were falling asleep. You have no need to worry or be afraid. The peace and calm that you are feeling now is the Spirit of God testifying to you these things are true. They are true, my dear friend, they are true."

All in the room had listened intently, without interruption.

They too were hearing these truths for the very first time, and they were visibly touched.[5] They had felt some things they had never felt before. The judge appeared cheerful and happy, as did the others, and all experienced a brief moment of complete and total solemnity.

The spiritual rejoicing experienced by all in the room was broken by a gentle knock at the door. Rebecca had fended off inquiries as to Willard's whereabouts long enough and had sent a messenger to retrieve him back to the farewell celebration.

"Please forgive my departure, Judge. There are some people waiting for me and I must not delay my joining them any longer. I must bid you farewell."

Willard extended his hand for the last time to a man he loved as a brother. Judge Sawyer locked his feeble hand with Willard's and immediately burst into tears, not wanting to let go. Tears could be seen on Willard's cheeks as he brought his left hand forward to completely encircle Judge Sawyer's hand.

"I will see you soon, dear friend, in another place, and we will continue this conversation."

Willard pulled himself away from a man he respected and loved. It seemed to Willard that he had shed more tears in this one week than all the rest of his life combined.

"It is all right to cry," Willard said to himself as he walked back to the banquet being held in his honor. "It is all right to cry."

It was near 11 p.m. when he returned and the hall was still filled with people not wanting to say goodbye. Rebecca had

---

5 *Willard Washington Bean Autobiography*, 2:38. Bean further records that two months later Judge Sawyer passed away peacefully in his sleep. President Heber J. Grant had carried on correspondence with the judge folling his speaking at the Angel Moroni dedication. Following the death of Judge Sawyer, President Grant wrote to the judge's daughter seeking permission to do his temple work. She consulted with the rest of the family members and they gave their consent for his temple ordinances to be done.

endeared herself to so many through her work as Relief Society President. She had offered her services tirelessly to every women's and service organization in the Palmyra area and had used her musical talents at almost every old folks' gathering in the area. She had become one with them and could now claim more friends than anyone else in Wayne County.

Willard and Rebecca awakened the next morning to finish packing their recently acquired 8-cylinder Pontiac. Willard could hardly wait to get it on the open stretches out west to see if it would break the sound barrier at 40 miles per hour.

Willard walked past the phone that had rung constantly for the past week as he tried to get out the door with another load of boxes. He dropped his boxes in a heap on the floor and picked up the receiver.

"Mr. Bean, this is Lute Sheldon, down here at the diner. I know you are packing up and getting ready to go and probably haven't had time to fix breakfast. It would afford me great satisfaction and a high favor if you and Mrs. Bean would have your last meal with me at my diner?"[6]

"Lute, that is awful nice of you, and you are right," Willard said. "We have not had time to eat any breakfast this morning. I am sure we would be delighted to share a table with you for our last meal in Palmyra. We can be there in about a half an hour or so."

"What are your favorite meals, Willard, and I'll have them ready by the time you get here?"

"Eggs over easy with some of your good pork sausage and some hashed browns would make me smile real big. As for my wife, she says hot cereal and milk will be just fine."

"Ha!" laughed Lute. "I'll tell you right now, she's going to get more than that."

---

[6] *Willard Washington Bean Autobiography*, 2:38

"Thanks, Lute. You're always so good to us. We'll see you in a bit."

Willard smashed the last box of clothing into place in the back seat of the Pontiac and slammed the door tight to keep it all in relative order. He turned around and saw Rebecca staring aimlessly, one last time, at the home that had been theirs for over 24 years. They were all out of tears, having gone to the well many times during the past week as they bid their farewells.

"My dear, let's go get that free breakfast we've been working for since we came here. I think you deserve it. Then, we'll head west and hope that there is something for old people like us to do back there."

"Funny, isn't it?" Rebecca said as they looked westward toward the Sacred Grove one last time. "When we first arrived we couldn't buy a meal from anyone, let alone any food. Now they are buying meals for us. I think they like us now, and I know how much I love them. My dear, I think we have made a friend or two. I really think we have. We have done all we know how to do and a little more, I suppose. It is time for us to be getting on home."

EPILOGUE

Willard and Rebecca came home to Salt Lake City and never returned to Palmyra. While they were in New York they were instrumental in bringing the Hill Cumorah, the Martin Harris Farm, and the Peter Whitmer farm under the ownership of the Church. They left a legacy of friendship and good will among the people of Palmyra never to be forgotten.

Willard served the remainder of his life as a missionary guide on Temple Square until his death on September 25, 1949. The local newspaper quoted him as saying, "It used to be Kid Bean; next it was Willard Bean; then Mr. Bean; and in some places, Brother Bean; then the Fighting Parson; now Old Man Bean; and yet a little longer my friends who call to see me will say, well—'he looks natural;' and then . . . well, I'll just take my place along with the long line of forgotten men."[1]

Rebecca Rosetta Peterson Bean worked in the temple while her health permitted. Following her husband's death, she lived alone for twenty-seven years. For most of those years she would annually speak at more than 100 firesides and Church gatherings, sharing her and her husband's experiences on the Joseph Smith farm.

As her life drew to a close she said, "My days and nights in the sunset of my life are sweet and peaceful and filled with golden memories. I have such love for all the missionaries I have

---

[1] *Bean Scrapbook*

known. I was 'Mom' to thousands of missionaries, and I could never live long enough to thank my Father in Heaven for all the blessings that I have had in my life and that are mine today." [2]

She passed away on June 25, 1976.

After Willard's death, President George Albert Smith wrote the following letter:

Willard Washington Bean
1868 - 1949

"I congratulate the life and family of Willard Bean. You have one of the best husbands and fathers in all the world. He has continued to lay up treasures in heaven where nobody can take them from him. And if each of you who belong to him will follow his example, you will do everything you can to make your mother happy, and, in due time you will all be reunited in the Celestial Kingdom of our Father when this earth becomes that kingdom.

I've loved Willard as a brother and I extend to you sincere condolence and sympathy at this time and pray that the Lord will bestow upon all of you His spirit, that your hearts may be comforted and that you may labor together to continue the work which Willard devoted his life.

Affectionately, Your Brother in the Gospel,

George Albert Smith [3]

---

[2] Rebecca Bean Fireside talk, 1964.
[3] Letter from President George Albert Smith, read by LeGrand Richards at the Funeral of Willard Bean.

Rebecca Rosetta Peterson Bean
1891 – 1976

Before she passed away, Rebecca wrote this letter:

August 26, 1953

My dearest children,

When you read this I will be gone. But there must be no sorrow. Death has to come as well as birth. I hope my love and my influence will be round about you as long as you live.

Remember always this life is only a preparation for the life to come, so live it well and be proud of your heritage. Gain a strong testimony of the gospel and do not fail to get your temple work done.

I have loved you deeply with the love that only mothers know. I haven't much to leave you except my love and a testimony that is humble and sincere. The Prophet Joseph is as real to me as any living person I have ever known, and there will be a friendship deep between us few earthly friends have known.

My testimony of the Savior is sacred and glorious for I have seen Him, heard His voice and felt the touch of His hand. Life has been good to me—better than I have ever deserved.

Be kind and helpful to each other, and love one another as I have loved you. Until we meet again, my love everlasting.

Your devoted Mother [4]

---

4 This letter was written by Rebecca Bean to her chilren in 1953, long before her death, with instructions to not open it until she passed away.

Rand H. Packer

ABOUT THE AUTHOR

As a young boy, Rand H. Packer often spent time with his grandparents, Willard and Rebecca Bean. It was from them, and from his mother Palmyra, that he nourished an avid interest in the history and happenings of the restoration of the gospel in the land of Cumorah.

Following his mission to New Zealand, he pursued a 36-year career in the Church Educational System. During that time he received a MA degree from Brigham Young University in LDS Church History and Doctrine, writing a thesis on "Four Mormon Landmarks in Western New York."

Speaking engagements have taken him many places throughout the United States and Canada, and his writings have found publication with Bookcraft, Deseret Book, and the *New Era.*

Rand is a frequent guest lecturer at Church and educational gatherings such as BYU and BYU-Idaho Education Weeks.

He is currently the CEO of Spouse Spice LLC, a business that is dedicated to strengthening and enhancing marriage relationships.

Rand and his wife Shirlee have nine children: Trevor, Cameron, Chipman, Spencer, Matthew, Tiffany, TJ, Shalayne, and Celisa.

BIBLIOGRAPHY

Bean, Rebecca Rosetta Peterson, *An Account of the Palmyra Missionary Experiences of Willard W. Bean and Rebecca P. Bean*, Palmyra Bean Packer Collection, Provo, Utah.

"Personal History, (blue note book)," Palmyra Bean Packer Collection, Provo, Utah.

"Fireside Talk, Salt Lake City, Utah, 1964." Recording and transcript in Palmyra Bean Packer Collection, Provo, Utah.

Bean, Willard Washington, *Autobiography of Willard Washington Bean*, Palmyra Bean Packer Collection, Provo, Utah.

"Willard Bean Scrapbook." MSS 298, no. 38. copy #1, L. Tom Perry Special Collections, Harold B. Lee Library, Brigham Young University, Provo, Utah.

Correspondence to Presiding Bishopric, 1915-1939. Archives of The Church of Jesus Christ of Latter-day Saints, Salt Lake City, Utah.

Correspondence with 1st Presidency and Presiding Bishopric, Palmyra Bean Packer Collection.

"Epitome of Activities in Palmyra, New York." In the Palmyra Bean Packer Collection, Provo, Utah.

Boone, David F. *Palmyra Revisited: The New York Mission of Willard W. and Rebecca P. Bean*, Brigham Young University, Department of Church History and Doctrine, Regional Studies in Latter-day Saint Church History, 2002.

Cook, Thomas L. *Palmyra and Vicinity*, L. Tom Perry Special Collections, Harold B. Lee Library, Brigham Young University, Provo, Utah.

Packer, Cameron J. *A Study of the Hill Cumorah: A Significant Latter-day Saint Landmark in Western New York.* Master's Thesis, Brigham Young University, 2002.

Packer, Palmyra Bean, *A Life Sketch of Palmyra Bean Packer*, Palmyra Bean Packer Collection.

Packer, Rand H. *The History of Four Mormon Landmarks in Western New York: The Joseph Smith Farm, Hill Cumorah, the Martin Harris Farm, and the Peter Whitmer, Sr. Farm.* Master's Thesis, Brigham Young University, 1975.

Porter, Larry C. *A Study of the Origins of The Church of Jesus Christ of Latter-day Saints in the States of New York and Pennsylvania, 1816-1831.* (Ph.D. dissertation, Brigham Young University, 1971).

Stevenson, Edward. *Reminiscences of Joseph, the Prophet, and the Coming Forth of the Book of Mormon.* Salt Lake City: Edward Stevenson, 1893.

Topliff, Vicki Bean, *Willard Bean, The Fighting Parson*, 1981.

The Life History of Alvin Pliny Bean, 2006.

Transcript, 1949. *The Funeral Service of Willard Washington Bean*, Palmyra Bean Packer Collection.

68725125R00109

Made in the USA
Middletown, DE
17 September 2019